PRELUDE TO
SUEZ

Detail from picture on p. 70. (*Mirrorpix*)

PRELUDE TO
SUEZ

ROBERT HORNBY

AMBERLEY

To foreign correspondents who risk everything for the facts.

First published 2010

Amberley Publishing Plc
Cirencester Road, Chalford,
Stroud, Gloucestershire, GL6 8PE

www.amberley-books.com

Copyright © Robert Hornby 2010

The right of Robert Hornby to be identified as the Author
of this work has been asserted in accordance with the
Copyrights, Designs and Patents Act 1988.

British Library Cataloguing in Publication Data.
A catalogue record for this book is available from the British Library.

ISBN 978 1 84868 864 3

Typeset in 10pt on 12pt Sabon.
Typesetting and Origination by FONTHILLDESIGN.
Printed in the UK.

Contents

Cairo Burns on Day of Riots

26 January 1952 became known in Egypt as Black Saturday. It was a day of arson and rioting in Cairo, resulting in the immediate deaths of two Englishmen: one, dragged from the Turf Club in the centre of the city, was murdered, his body dismembered and burnt in the street; the other, cornered trying to escape by jumping from an upstairs window of the Club, was caught and hacked to death. The Canadian Trade Commissioner, also escaping from the Club, was later found stabbed to death. Two days later, the British Ambassador informed the Egyptian Government of these deaths. The eventual death toll after the weeks of rioting was put at seventeen British and other nationals living in Cairo. No 'official' figures were ever released by the Egyptian Government.

Buildings associated with the British presence were burnt to the ground. Barclays Bank, British Overseas Airways Corporation offices, four cinemas, petrol stations and night clubs were some of the targets mentioned to me by correspondents, as well as, to their regret, their favourite bars. Any shop or club selling alcohol was sure to be burnt by a mob stirred up by the Moslem Brotherhood.

The last to go up was Shepheard's Hotel, in its day as famous as Raffles in Singapore. American correspondents, whose watering hole this had become, were given front-row seats on the terrace to watch the Badia night club go up in flames – that is until the fire which had been lit in the back of Shepheard's by the rioters had reached the front of the hotel. The press fled. As the British Military Spokesman in Cairo, my office had been besieged up to then by the mainly British press corps. Some elements of the American press had been hostile towards the British position in Egypt. When they arrived in my office, there was a change of mood. In particular, a well-known woman columnist, who had only been able to rescue her fur coat and the very little she was wearing at the time (this she proved by opening her coat wide for my benefit) asked 'why the hell weren't we doing something about the rioting.' It was of little use at this stage to say that the lukewarm support for the British presence in Egypt by the American press had probably also encouraged Nahas Pasha and the Wafd, back in power in October 1951, to stir up the revolutionary undercurrents in Cairo and Alexandria. They were demanding the withdrawal of British troops, whether in uniform or not, from the Egyptian delta. Confined as they were to the Canal Zone, any overt action to protect British or, for that matter, American nationals in Cairo would have meant re-occupation. Little did I know how near things would come to this later that day.

During the few months I had been briefing the press in Cairo, I had established telephone links with the GHQ of the British command using the local telephone exchange and routing my calls through Ismailia to the garrison town of Moascar, the army base. This worked the whole time I was in Cairo, but it was vulnerable and insecure. So I had rigged up an aerial to a convenient tree in the British Embassy garden, connected to an army 22 wireless transmitter, the reliable and standard issue during the war. With this I was in voice contact with my opposite number in the Canal Zone. My call sign was 'Haybox'. This was only to be used if the go ahead had been given for the British forces to re-occupy Cairo. I would then brief the Cairo press on what was happening. The Embassy itself was protected by the Egyptian army mainly because of the nearby houses of the Prime Minister, Nahas Pasha, and the Minister of the Interior, Serag el Din.

If Sir Ralph Stevenson, the British Ambassador, had triggered the intervention of the army, the 16th Independent Parachute Brigade, recently arrived in the Canal Zone, would have been landing on the Gezira Club Polo Ground followed by armoured vehicles pouring in on the desert road from the Canal Zone. The re-occupation of Egypt by British forces would have been set in motion. The deadline for military action was 5.00 p.m. After that, darkness would have made parachute drops a nightmare and tanks negotiating narrow streets a chaos.

My wife and two children were in a flat in Zamalek, the favoured residential district for the British some two miles from the Embassy; this was another likely target for the arsonists. I asked myself, do I stay in the Embassy garden and do my duty, or do I rescue my family? I was relieved of that decision by being summoned to the Ambassador's study where a number of staff were meeting to discuss calling in the army, the very step I had been ready to implement. It became clear that the Egyptian army had not yet been called to restore order and the police were taking very little notice of the activities of the rioters. It was reported that the Assistant Commander of Police, Imam Bey, had watched the Rivoli Cinema being torched while standing nearby with his hands in his pockets. When approached by an Egyptian citizen asking why he was doing nothing he replied, 'Let

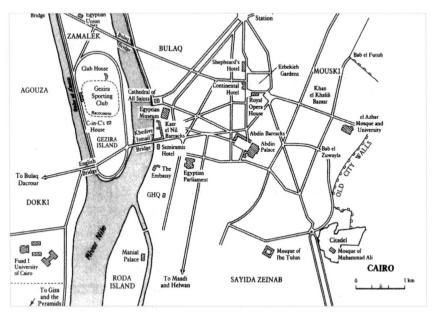

Map of Cairo in the early 1950s.

the boys have their fun'.[1] But while I was at this crucial meeting, reports came in that there was a strong police presence in the area of the Semiramis Hotel, less than half a mile from the Embassy and Prime Minister Nahas Pasha's house. Then it was flashed that some rioters, attempting to get into the hotel entrance, had been stopped and one shot dead by the police. There was then a cessation of rioting according to the messages arriving at the Embassy and it seemed as if the worst might be over. Clearly some Egyptian military action had been called for. I packed up my good old 22 wireless set with considerable relief, took a car and drove to Zamalek to find my wife and the English friend who had come to stay with us playing charades to keep the children happy, whilst the dying flames from Cairo City could still be seen in the distance. The next day revealed the true horrors of the twelve hours when the Government had not only lost control, but had encouraged one outrage after another. The British Embassy later reported ten deaths alone in the vicinity of the Turf Club. The damage throughout the city was estimated at £20 million to £50 million at 1952 prices. Some 10–15,000 workers were to be put out of work. Later it was announced that King Farouk had declared Martial Law throughout Egypt.

Sitting in my office late that night with many of the foreign correspondents who were to become close friends in the months ahead, I asked myself how I had come to put my wife and children in such danger. Had we not done enough during the war?

CHAPTER ONE

The Start of it All

It had all started one day in 1946 when I was sitting comfortably in the old War Office, which was opposite the Cenotaph in Whitehall, hardly believing my luck. Burma and the battles of Kohima, Mandalay and even Rangoon seemed as far away as they really were. I had a flat in Kensington, a beautiful wife and two girls, aged five and one – the 'war gap'. A green uniformed War Office 'messenger' had just opened the door to my snug office and asked if my fire needed attention. Those were certainly the days which a modern soldier in the Ministry of Defence would not believe.

When the door opened again it was no 'messenger', at least, not in one sense of the word, but Lieutenant-General Sir Arthur Dowler, the Colonel of the East Surreys, the regiment to which I had had the privilege of being commissioned into as a regular officer during the War. 'What are you doing here Hornby?' If I had answered honestly I would have said, 'enjoying myself and all that peace seemed to be offering.' What 'Pop' Dowler (as he was known throughout the service) said, quite shortly, was that he had been appointed GOC East Africa and wanted someone on his staff who could deal with the local press, intransigent British settlers and visiting foreign correspondents. It was an immense command covering five colonies. It so happened that, as I had been downgraded physically, regimental soldiering was

The author, 1962, on his retirement from the army.

out and my job in the Whitehall press office was considered a 'cosy' option. This was no doubt the reason why I was being posted to see what I could do to improve press and local public relations in Nairobi and East Africa. One does not argue with generals; I was soon at sea in the troop ship *Empire Ken*, bound for Mombasa.

The sea journey took over six weeks with diversions to Greece and Mogadishu, the port of Somalia. This wartime ship had been one of Hitler's 'joy ships', renamed after capture by the Royal Navy. Hitler used them to reward favoured officers and their girlfriends with cruises to the Fiords. However, when the ship was captured the German Captain had sabotaged the stabiliser with the result that she now sailed with a permanent fifteen degree list. This only became apparent when one disembarked and tried to walk upright on the nearest dockside pavement. Male officers were four to a cabin with wives and children incarcerated in cabins on the lower decks.

To arrive at Mombasa by ship is to experience at once the excitement of Africa. While Port Said is cosmopolitan, Mombasa conjures up all that one has ever read about the 'dark continent'. In 1949, Arab Dhows were still to be seen in plenty. Boarding the East African Railways and Harbours train, as it was then named, was an exciting business. Only recently had dining cars been added, thus avoiding the wayside stops for *ad hoc* meals which I had become used to in India. The feeling of adventure was heightened by the friendly jostling crowds of African families, turbaned Sikhs and sari clad Indian women, and mixing with them all the children of settlers meeting up with families, and not least our own two wide-eyed and excited girls.

It was a long overnight journey in those days, but enhanced during daylight hours by views of wild game at short distances. At most stops monkeys were thrust into the windows by vendors hoping for a sale before the train moved off once again. So it was with some relief to get the children off at Nairobi station where the same colourful crowds jostled for seats for the next stage of their journey into Uganda.

For us it was to be a night at the Nairobi Club en route for the Brackenhurst Hotel in Limuru, some thirty miles from Nairobi, and the Headquarters of East Africa Command just outside Nairobi, where I was to have my office close to the GOC and his staff. It was also the first night for a wartime family to see and eat food which had been off the dining table for five years but which was now weighing down two billiard tables set for a buffet. There was everything one had imagined eating but never had for those long years of war; we revelled in it.

The peace in East Africa had been kept between warring factions by British and African troops supporting the District Officers; the former being regiments of the King's African Rifles, some eight battalions. This was a formidable and well-disciplined force commanded by British officers and comprising soldiers from the various tribal groups. Seeing the turmoil, death, and destruction taking place in former colonies today, it is hard to make those who denigrated our occupation of those vast territories believe that their populations lived in harmony for the most part, in plenty, and in security under the paternalistic ethos of the old Colonial Office. But, of course, there was resentment among the Africans who had received their education at British schools and universities at this patronising assumption that they did not wish for independence and the removal of British commanded troops from their homelands. They were to be greatly encouraged by Harold Macmillan's 'Wind of Change' speech, when the Conservatives achieved office again in 1951. The magnitude of this concept can best be judged by the similar magnitude of the populations involved. The East African Colonies, for which the GOC had military responsibilities for security, were well in excess of some thirty million people.[1]

Taking up my duties to lessen this resentment, which was not only from the indigenous African but also the white settlers who had come to look upon the land as their own forever, I was grateful for the wise guidance then of George Kinnear, editor of the *East African Standard*. He had been a former war correspondent covering the Italian invasion of British Somaliland in 1940, successfully repulsed by East African, South African and Nigerian Brigades who had then moved into Italian Somaliland, capturing Mogadishu. He understood soldiers and the military and civilian problems facing General 'Pop' Dowler, the GOC of this vast region. My first tasks were to find somewhere to live other than a hotel thirty miles from my office, and to get the children into a school. The army in those days expected officers and particularly their wives just to get on with it, with as little financial help as the Treasury could achieve through the use of their Byzantine regulations. So within

General 'Pop' Dowler, GOC East African Command.

a few weeks, we had rented a house right on the edge of suburban Nairobi at Kiambu, one step from being in the bush and an easy daily drive to GHQ, and my eldest daughter was enrolled at 'Kenya High'. Our then five Kikuyu 'boys' lived in an adjoining kraal. We had been shocked at the low wages and provision only of 'posho' or mealies, the staple African diet. We couldn't raise their wages without incurring the wrath of neighbouring settlers, so in addition we gave them basic needs such as soap, meat, sugar, salt and matches, the latter being vital as all our cooking and hot water depended upon wood fires. We were a happy little group with the nanny we had brought out with us on the troop ship. A stickler for routine and brought up in Scotland, she would dress in full Kensington Gardens rig for the afternoon walk, with our youngest in a pram and elder sister walking alongside, straight down the nearest jungle path. On one occasion my daughter remembers an African woman cowering ahead making gestures for them to stop. Nanny did not stop, and lifted the pram wheels to go over the 'log' lying right across the dirt road. As my daughter lifted her foot to step over it, the enormous black mamba stretching the width of the 'road' suddenly moved off into the jungle! Luckily no-one was hurt on this occasion.

As I was to experience in my later 'postings' starting with Cairo, I had only to arrive somewhere and a crisis would follow. So it was in Kenya. Although we had experienced nothing but respect from the Africans with whom we had had contact and, in some cases, made friends with, an underground movement for the recovery of lands owned by settlers, many of whom had been induced to come to Kenya to farm under generous Government provisions, was inflamed by the revolutionary leader Jomo Kenyatta. At first he recruited mainly within the tribal reserves and the settlers' traditional way of life, with their African staffs, continued unabated. Lord Delamere's statue remained undefiled staring down and dominating Nairobi's main street. What was not known was the means of binding all Kenyans to the 'movement' by a fearsome Mau Mau oath, embodying every form of witchcraft and blood ritual. It was considered so shocking that when the details became known on the declaration of the 'emergency' in 1952, they were never published in the press, and access even to this day can only be obtained by a Member of Parliament with access to the House of Commons library.

In its early stages the oath spread rapidly among the Kikuyu everywhere, including among domestic servants and those working on British-owned farms. In addition to its declared aim of ridding the British from African lands, the oath involved such terrifying ritualistic acts that the effect on any African forced to take it was terrifying and irrevocable. It licensed acts of violence against those deemed to be occupying their land and embraced putting everyone at risk. From the start, my wife and children, living in the bush with only one house nearby, were in serious danger. My army .38 revolver was always in my wife's hands while I was in Nairobi at GHQ. This, and our pair of brindle danes that might give fair warning of anyone approaching the house by day or night, were our only defence.

But nothing then seemed to disturb the pleasant life of the 'old hands', epitomised by the Happy Valley crowd with their dances at the Muthaiga Club until dawn and their Agricultural Shows in Nanyuki. The army was not to be seen in any great way in Nairobi itself, and was still only acting in 'aid of the civil power' as needed. At the time it seemed there were adequate military and police reserves, and the Mau Mau movement had yet to claim the life of any white settler. As a precaution, however, the movement was officially banned in 1950. This was the same year that Nairobi celebrated becoming a city. Half a century before, one Sergeant Ellis of the Royal Engineers pitched his camp, exhausted, having built the rail road from Mombasa, leaving him in financial arrears on behalf of the War Office. His camp was a site described by R. O. Preston in 1899 as 'A bleak swampy stretch of soggy landscape, wind swept and devoid of human habitation'.[2] It was the site of the future city, in the very heart of the Kikuyu tribal lands.

It was soon after the celebrations that my wife and I woke one morning to a strange silence – no early morning tea, no sounds from the kitchen. A brief look revealed empty living quarters and not an African 'boy' in sight. Police enquiries about these missing members of what we considered our 'family' were met with the comment that they had no doubt taken the Mau Mau oath and had left us rather than be called upon to use their pangas against us. We were lucky said the Inspector. Soon afterwards there was an attack on a family by one of their most trusted house boys who had served dinner quite normally until the third course, whereupon he produced a panga and slaughtered the family. As soon as we could we moved into Nairobi; it had become easier to find rented accommodation as people had begun to leave. One of our African servants from Kiambu, the 'shamba' (garden boy), turned up to rejoin us and was instantly promoted to become the house boy. This term, 'boy', was widely used but hurtful to Africans, degrading their manhood, and we tried not to use it in conversation.

We enjoyed living in the city with all its amenities. Not least of these comforts was our proximity to Kenya High, our daughter's school, and St Andrew's church, which put on a weekly highland dance which our very Scottish nanny *had* to attend. It saved me the long drive from Kiambu to the city as I always took her there and waited. We were not to know how quickly the situation would deteriorate; a state of emergency directly involving the army would soon occur.

In early 1951, I received a call from the Director of Public Relations of Middle East Command stationed in the Canal Zone to say that he was coming to Nairobi to talk to me. He said when we met that he wanted me in Cairo to improve press relations with the resident and visiting foreign correspondents and, not least, the anti-British Arab press. I was to work closely with the Information Department of the British Embassy. He stifled my murmurings about finishing the job in East Africa by telling me that I was being given a temporary rank of Lieutenant-Colonel. It was symptomatic of the immediate post-war years that I had come back from Burma with the rank of Major. This was reduced to my substantive rank of Captain upon rejoining my regiment, only to be promoted again to Major on being posted to Kenya. Now I was to be a Lieutenant-Colonel at the age of 31. I was to live in Cairo, wearing mufti (civilian clothes), with my wife and family, but also have an office at GHQ Fayid in the Canal Zone, where I was to be Assistant Director of Public Relations.

CHAPTER TWO

From Kenya to Cairo
1951–1953

It was to be the *Empire Ken* again from Mombasa, but hopefully a rather more comfortable voyage than the last as I was the senior officer aboard for the short journey to Port Said, the rail head for Cairo. This time we did feel the list as we disembarked into a bum boat to be taken to the dockside. Someone used one of the 'heads' on our side of the gangway with the resultant near misses of the deluge; some welcome to Port Said. I had been told it was the *entrepot* of the Middle East, with the emphasis on the last syllable I had to agree! It had been a dreadful journey. Although I was SOB, Senior Officer on Board, I was still separated from my wife and children, who had to share a cabin with another wife and four children between them, while I bunked up with a fellow officer in a single cabin. However, it was so hot and humid over the ten days' journey from Mombasa that we slept on deck when we could. This was standard troop ship accommodation in the war, but I thought the War Office could have made better allowance in peace time for families. We certainly did not travel POSH (Port Out Starboard Home), the pre-war Indian army slang for officers with a bit of money who booked the expensive cabins on the shady port side for the long sea trip to Bombay, and the equally cool starboard side on their return to the UK. 'Are you travelling POSH?' was the accepted put-down. Strange how this has now become common usage with few aware of what it meant originally.

Port Said was then the major port for supplying the British forces stationed in the Canal Zone under the Anglo-Egyptian Treaty of 1936 and the Sudan Agreement of 1899. A major concession of the Treaty was that British personnel were allowed to reside or visit Cairo and Alexandria carrying only a Forces Identity Card. Neither a passport, nor a visa was required. Uniform could be worn, though the majority of soldiers stationed in Cairo chose not to wear it. This concession was the first to be revoked by Prime Minister Nahas Pasha as relations between the British and Egyptian Governments deteriorated, resulting in the abrogation of the treaty in October 1951 where he declared that all British army soldiers and their dependents were to leave Cairo and Alexandria or face arrest and imprisonment. The Moslem Brotherhood and revolutionary movements within the Egyptian Government pressed for the evacuation of all troops from Egypt, including the Canal Zone. In 1951 this would have meant closing the Canal Zone base and ending British influence throughout the Middle East.

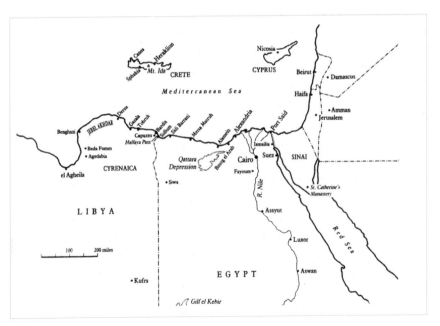

Map of Egypt showing the Canal Zone north of Suez.

Upon our arrival at Port Said in that summer of 1951, little knowing what was to come and with typical colonial nonchalance, all I presented to obtain the right to take a train to Cairo with my wife and family and cases of personal effects was a small Forces Identity Card, not even showing a photograph. I was also unaware of how soon the calm cooperation of porters employed by a British officer at Cairo station would be shattered. My last impression of what had once been a symbol of our colonial superiority was a line of some twenty 'fellaheen' (tillers of the soil), now railway porters, following a white woman and two young girls down the length of the platform laden with tea chests and trunks, the traditional army containers for household belongings.

Unlike the Diplomatic Corps, who are given a selection of villas or flats according to rank from which to choose, army officers are expected to make their own arrangements for accommodation unless a married quarter is available. Our selection, *force majeure*, was a guest house in Zamalek, while we would continue to look for a flat we could afford to rent as a permanent residence for the duration of my posting.

The news of my arrival did not take long to come to the notice of the Cairo press; I began to answer press questions as a British Military Spokesman. During the war, Cairo had been GHQ of the Middle East Forces and where the desert campaigns had been planned. Unlike in Britain, there had been no 'black out' until Rommel was practically at the door, and there had been no shortage of good food; the Cairo social life followed an endless round. The city's reputation for gossip, political upheaval and an extravagant nightlife ensured the continued presence of foreign correspondents and city based news agencies; it was a magnet for war correspondents, commentators, writers and, as one would say today, celebrities from countries caught up in the conflict. Although the number of correspondents fluctuated with the number of crises, the BBC in particular had permanent offices practically next door to the Embassy. These offices were used by some lesser members of the Embassy staff and indeed, were where I found myself.

I became something of a problem to those who liked to slot people by rank, accent and function. An important British Embassy to this day has two Military Attachés: the senior, a Brigadier, and the junior, a Major. The senior post was often awarded towards the end of service as compensation for some miserable former postings, and, for the junior officer, the post was granted to provide experience in the workings of the Foreign Office. Both ranks in Cairo were heartily welcomed socially at the continuous round of cocktail and dinner parties in the tradition of diplomatic life, but who was I? A Lieutenant-Colonel out ranking the junior attaché, Major Peter Tamlyn, whose social graces and knowledge of Debretts were second to none. There was natural resentment. Then, as someone who 'dealt with the press', it was not easy to enter the gilded circle, even if my wife and I chose to. But the correspondents had different views. For them the Canal Zone, which could still be visited when I arrived, was a tiring journey over a desert road, or through endless crowded small towns to reach Ismailia, and from there to GHQ at Fayid. The Cable and Wireless offices in Cairo provided facilities to file stories to the U.K. and worldwide, but were restricted outside Cairo to Port Said and Suez. To be able to put questions and get comments from a Military Spokesman in Cairo was a bonus. No need to leave one of the press 'haunts' or be out of Cairo and perhaps miss the unfolding crises as successive Government appointees rose and fell at the whim of King Farouk. I was made welcome.

Two Arabic papers, the so-called semi-independent *Al Ahram* and the *Gamal hour El Misr*, provided vicious anti-British stories of imagined misdeeds by the British army, which newly-arrived correspondents sometimes sent, without checking with me, to their foreign desks prefacing the 'story' with the source, usually one of these two papers. This was an acceptable practice up to a point, when there was no one available to check. Now I was there it was up to me to put the other side and give the facts. My civil telephone line to the Canal Zone and GHQ via Ismailia/Moascar was invaluable and quick. Very often, by making a statement to Reuters in Cairo, my rebuttal of a sensational *El Misr* story would reach the foreign desk of a daily paper before their own correspondent's 'copy'. This had only to happen once or twice before they checked with me before sending a cable with a sensational account of the misdoings of the army. Later, as attacks on the army became more intense, it was even more vital to get the truth out quickly and for me to give an accurate account. When censorship was eventually imposed by the Egyptian Government on the Cable and Wireless offices, I had already established a communication route through which I could telephone correspondents' copies to their papers via the Royal Signals Regiment at GHQ. I did this by getting my Arabic speaking clerk to ask for the Egyptian civil exchange at Ismailia, and once through, asking in turn for 'Moascar', the military exchange for the whole of the Canal Zone and GHQ. This gave me direct access to my boss, Colonel 'Jock' Carroll, who had yanked me out of Kenya. I then had a typist at GHQ who took down from me the correspondent's despatch to his office. This was sent by Royal Signals to the press branch in the War Office from where it was picked up by a relevant newspaper messenger. But all that was to come. During my first few weeks in the summer of 1951, though the situation was tense, life went on as normal and I met socially and at my Embassy office most of the permanent Cairo based press, and occasionally a visiting 'fireman'.

The system I put in practice was to set up daily press conferences around five or six o'clock in the evening, when most had recovered from the afternoon siesta. Embassy hours and those of most of the British firms were from eight or nine o'clock in the morning to one o'clock in the afternoon, and re-opening after the traditional siesta. This allowed some work to be done before the evening round of diplomatic parties. That time suited most of the press for a round up of the day's news, particularly Patrick Smith, the BBC Middle East correspondent, whose studio was in the same building outside the Embassy compound but within the diplomatic area and fairly safe. In September 1951, when news was relatively quiet, I used to 'sit in' with him as he used his open line to Bush House, London, to read his despatch for the evening news. While waiting to go 'On Air', we could hear the tinkle of tea cups as the girls in Broadcasting House chatted, waiting to put Patrick on the air, and the grinding sound of the London Buses going past. An uncanny reminder of a life my wife and I had left behind. There was to be another when we were asked to go with a diplomatic party to Cairo airport to watch the new fabulous jet airliner, the 'Comet', land on its inaugural flight round the world. It came down on a sultry Cairo night, with ice still on its wings, to cheers and clapping and the amazement of us all. Could any of us have imagined that this plane's basic design would result in it being adopted by the Royal Air Force, after twenty-five years of civil flying, then be renamed the Nimrod, and twenty-five years later be used in trooping from Iraq and Afghanistan?

Detail from picture on p. 51. (*Mirrorpix*)

CHAPTER THREE

The Abrogation of the Anglo-Egyptian Treaty and the Start of the Propaganda War

On 3 September 1951, the Egyptian Government claimed the right to block the Suez Canal to sea traffic bound for Haifa, a corollary of its dispute with the newly created state of Israel, which had been getting its vital oil supplies through the Canal Zone route. This was all part of a sustained attack by the Arab League. The actions were condemned by a resolution of the Security Council of the United Nations and the waterways were kept open. *El Misr*, the leading Cairo daily paper, declared that the American and British actions at the Security Council Meeting 'would plunge not only the Middle East but the whole world into war.' This was the rhetoric which increased almost daily as the situation worsened; Cairo once again became a centre for the world press covering the Middle East. On 14 September, Dr Mooussadek, Prime Minister of Persia (Iran) in the days of the Shah, sent an ultimatum to the British Government demanding the expulsion of the oil experts, and then dropped it pending the election results in Britain. The Labour Government acted before the situation deteriorated and ordered the Shell staff to withdraw from Abadan. On 4 October, HMS *Mauritius* evacuated 250 staff.

This was to have a profound effect on the Egyptian situation. Nahas Pasha and the Wafd Party were firmly in power. Interned members of the Moslem Brotherhood had been released and a blind eye was turned to attacks on troops in the Canal Zone. The retreat from the Persian oil problem by the British Government was a green light for the revolutionary movement. On Monday 6 October 1951, Nahas Pasha tabled his decrees denouncing the Anglo-Egyptian Treaty of 1936 and the Condominium Agreement of 1899, whereby Sudan remained under British Administration. The condominium in effect was a joint sovereignty device, Farouk being King of Egypt and the British Monarch being ruler of Sudan. By declaring Farouk as King of Sudan, in effect annexing Sudan, Nahas Pasha curried favour with the King and stifled an American proposal that Egypt should become a 'co-equal partner' with Great Britain, France and Turkey in its projected Middle East Defence Organisation.[1]

A long term politician, Nahas Pasha had, by 1936, formed three Ministries in eight years and confronted Farouk's father, the authoritarian King Fuad, who had acceded to the signing of the 1936 Treaty with the blessing of the British Government in 1937. Nahas Pasha then challenged the young King Farouk's powers on accession for his own ends, but lost the premiership to Ali Maher for stirring

Prime Minister Nahas Pasha (left), leader of the Wafd party, with King Farouk in May 1951.

up riots. It was to be an ironic twist of fate that following 'Black Saturday' in January 1952, Nahas Pasha was again to be superseded by Ali Maher. But that was in the future. In October 1951, he sought to bring the revolutionary fervour of the Wafd to a head and drive British troops out of Egypt once and for all. His first step, therefore, was to abrogate the 1936 Treaty which allowed British troops to be in Cairo and Alexandria. His timing was carefully chosen; in October, the greater majority of the Embassy staff were away in Alexandria. This followed the established pattern of moving there during the hot months, following the custom in India when officer's families moved to hill stations and the Government transported itself to Simla. This seasonal absence was to create an immediate problem for the Embassy in its efforts to combat the wave of anti-British propaganda being organised by the Serag el Din Pasha, the Minister of the Interior and propagandist of the Wafd party. He would later also impose censorship.

The only means of communication between Cairo and Alexandria was by telephone via Egyptian exchanges in the same way that I had set up a line from Cairo to the Canal Zone. There was, of course, the Diplomatic Wireless Service (DWS), but that was too slow for the immediate rebuttal of the incandescent stories which had already induced crowds on the street to begin jostling British soldiers.

Cairo, rather than Alexandria, was the Middle East press centre during the 'hot months'. It created one advantage for the Embassy: the Information Department had not moved to Alexandria and was still sweating it out in Cairo. Heading up this department and responsible for combating anti-British propaganda was 'Roddy' Parkes, later Sir Roderick and Ambassador in Saigon. In Cairo he was Minister to the Embassy and the Ambassador's deputy. I had already started a comprehensive listing of the British and foreign press newcomers arriving by the minute to cover this major international story; the Embassy information people also had their list of local press and civilian contacts.

A press conference following Nahas Pasha's unilateral statement was hastily called at the Information Offices. At this, Roddy Parkes was to give a political reaction, while I reported on the position of the army in the Canal Zone and what effect Nahas Pasha's threats might have on the military presence in Cairo. I was soon to find out for myself. The questions came thick and fast.

It was not surprising that Roddy had little to say about the British Government's reaction, being, as he was, cut off from immediate consultation with the Embassy staff in Alexandria and the Foreign Office in London. Meanwhile, I was relaying the news from the Canal Zone through my telephone link. The guidance I was getting was not to inflame the situation by threatening or forecasting military action.

We were facing some thirty journalists, some whom had flown into Cairo, plus the resident press corps. Reuters had a staff of five headed by Haigh Nicholson, in competition with the Associated Press of America led by Fred Zuzy and Socratese Chakalas, 'Soc' to everyone. Agence France Presse was strongly represented by M. Dardaud. There was a sea of faces, many of whom I got to know well in the future. We did our best but the press did better and got out the news and comment that night, catching the press worldwide through the Cable and Wireless offices, still fully operational and not yet under the control of Serag el Din, the Foreign Minister.

One of the decisions we made early on was not to invite representatives of the Egyptian press, in particular the virulent anti-British *El Misr* and the so-called semi-independent *Al Ahram*. It would have done no good and the disruption and distortion of the answers to questions would have provided plenty of sensational copy for the other press listening, without much time for Roddy or myself to check and rebut what we knew would be fantasy but could not be left unchallenged.

During the following days the pattern of a joint daily press conference was established with someone from the Embassy to watch the political front. This was often Arthur Kellas, ex-Parachute Regiment, who had been invalided out and was now a second secretary of the Embassy. As the majority of the Embassy staff hastily made the return journey to Cairo, Roddy organised his extensive propaganda units, both overt and clandestine. I steered well clear of all that trying to establish a 'facts only' service to the resident and transitory press on the basis of which they could make their own assessment of the military situation. 'Spinning', if that meant playing one paper off against another to get a good story, was never attempted by me. What news I had went to every correspondent undiluted.

Anyone knowing the realities of international press coverage would not expect the news and comment always to be friendly to the British position or the activities of the army in the Canal Zone. The American press had a strong presence. *The New York Times*, led by Sirus Sulzberger, then probably the most well-known foreign correspondent of his time, had a team of five in the Middle East with a strong presence in Cairo. Their reporting, while not always favourable, was objective. Not the same could be said of the *New York Herald Tribune*, for whom at a later date the formidable Marguerite Higgins was reporting. In 1956, when the attempt was made to re-occupy the Suez Canal, the seeds were being sown for the critical attitude of the White House to future British action. The latent support of the American public for those they supposed had been exploited under colonial rule in the old British Empire was reflected in much of the reporting from the *Tribune*. On the other hand, The United Press of America – UP – did a straight forward job in getting out the news events and they often scooped other agencies in the first few weeks of October 1951. They too were heavily represented in Cairo and beyond. Even *Time Magazine*, the *Chicago Daily News* and *Chicago Herald* had representation. One concern was Larry Rue, Chief Middle East correspondent for the *Chicago Tribune* (one of the virulent anti-British Hearst newspapers) and a close friend of Abdul Fath, owner of *El Misr*. I was only to learn about this much later. Visits by these correspondents to the Canal Zone, where my public relations colleagues looked after them, were encouraged, but it was the exception when the offer was taken up, rather than the rule. Some did not want to be too associated with the British forces and preferred Cairo politics to the desert road.

That the British Government had been taken unawares by the rapid succession of events was clear. The abrogation of the 1936 Treaty was a triumph for Nahas Pasha and Serag el Din, the Foreign Minister, and it gave the Wafd a new lease of life.

Even *The Times* correspondent, whose meticulous reporting was to uphold the reputation of his paper as the outstanding journal of record, was bound to observe that Nahas Pasha had seized the right moment. I came to admire greatly *The Times* coverage as it was reported back to me from London. James Holburn, later to be made editor of the *Glasgow Herald*, was one of its correspondents in Cairo, and Tom Little another, who also produced the 'Arab News', a counter blast to the excesses of the Egyptian press and MENA (the

Middle East News Agency), producing a daily summary of the Arabic press, invaluable to my work and that of the Embassy. Their only by-line then was 'from our own correspondent' or 'from our diplomatic correspondent'.

It was *The Times* which had first revealed that the Egyptian Government had received conciliatory proposals from the British Foreign Secretary, backed by America, France and Turkey, for a joint Middle East Command, abruptly dismissed by the Wafd Party. It had been a valiant effort by Herbert Morrison, the Foreign Secretary of a Labour Government, even while fighting a General Election; the importance of stability in the Middle East and its potential as fighting 'cockpit' was recognised then as it is now.

But Nahas Pasha had wrong-footed them all by announcing the abrogation of the 1936 Treaty. When the Four Power proposals, led by Britain, were made public and rejected on 16 October, the impression given was that Britain had been the supplicant power, pleading a compromise for reconsideration. Having seized the initiative, no time was lost in stoking up the propaganda through the controlled Cairo press. The headlines in the Cairo papers said it all. 'King and People Break the Fetters of British Imperialism', 'Farouk, King of Egypt and Sudan', 'British Embassy Defies Egypt and Declares 1936 Treaty Still in Force'. With only a week having passed since Nahas Pasha had tabled his original decrees, the pressure on British interests, both political and commercial, was intense.

More correspondents arrived and the daily evening press conference was clearly too late to rebut the successive canards being written about the British forces in the Canal Zone, so they became twice daily. By mid-morning, thanks to Tom Little, I knew what was being said by *El Misr*, *Al Ahram* and the virulent mouth pieces of the Wafd and Moslem Brotherhood. The rebuttals from myself and from Roddy Parkes covering the political side were quickly transformed into communiqués distributed to all the known press and also to some 1000 British residents and prominent Egyptian contacts willing to receive them. The only way I could keep up with actions being taken in the Canal Zone and the reports in the UK press was to telephone through the worst of the Arabic press coverage and ask whether there was any truth in the stories, and then make a statement as the British Military Spokesman as though I was in the Canal Zone. The press corps played along with this, otherwise my tenure in Cairo was to be short lived, as indeed it became within a few weeks. In return I was starting my 'telephone service' for those who wanted to risk sending their copy direct and uncensored to their offices in London.

The final act in the abrogation procedures came on 15 October 1951, when the Chamber of Deputies approved the bills for the abrogation of the 1936 Treaty and the 1899 Sudan Condominium. What this did, causing me enormous difficulty, was to abolish the agreements under the 1936 Act which allowed British troops to visit Cairo, and for someone like myself with a formal appointment to reside there. There was now the threat of imprisonment if any army personnel were found in defiance of the Government Orders.

Wisely, GHQ had moved from Cairo to the Canal Zone in 1950. The second stage of isolating the British forces in the Canal Zone was about to begin. The implication of these measures taken by the Egyptian Government was that 'warlike acts', as *The Times* described them, could soon be taken against our forces with impunity, encouraged by the Wafd, with Moslem Brotherhood support. Calling a Brotherhood conference in Cairo, its spokesman demanded that Nahas Pasha 'declares war on Britain and the British forces'.[2] Nor was the growing crisis confined to the stand-off between Britain and Egypt. The United States, on 11 October, had condemned the unilateral actions of the Egyptian Government, an intervention simply ignored by Nahas Pasha. In the Sudan, however, 600 miles to the south of Cairo, there was fierce reaction to the fourth of Egypt's abrogation decrees, sweeping Sudan under the Kingship of Farouk. The UMMA Party in Sudan, which stood for complete independence, quickly issued a statement in the form of telegrams to the United Nations and the Foreign Ministers of both Britain and Egypt that 'the Sudan was not a party to the Agreements concluded by Britain and Egypt and has never recognised them'.[3] The statement went on to declare their sovereignty as an independent Sudan, and 'Egypt's efforts to impose on the SUDAN the Egyptian crown ... the greatest insult that Egypt has ever given the Sudan.' Using this Sudan decree was in fact another clever move by Nahas Pasha to put pressure on the British, knowing full well the strong feelings for independence expressed at the Assembly in Khartoum which had passed a resolution in December 1951, nine months earlier, demanding self-government.

Ibrahim Farag Pasha, Egypt's Foreign Minister, berated the British Government for questioning the legitimacy of the abrogation and condominium agreements, stating the Governor General in Sudan had now become 'an official of the Egyptian Government'. The British Foreign Secretary's response was robust. 'The Egyptians cannot have their cake and eat it' he declared. If Sudan demanded independence and freedom from foreign occupation, the Egyptian Government cannot say, at the same time, that this can only be achieved under the Egyptian Crown. The Foreign Secretary answered the claim by Ibrahim Farag Pasha that Egypt and the Sudan were 'one country and one people' by saying this was simply a miss-statement of fact. While some Northern Sudanese speak the same language and have the same religion so did Saudi Arabians, Iraqis and many others who once formed part of the Ottoman Empire. However, he then went a step further to say that only if the Sudanese, of their own free will, wanted union with Egypt 'His Majesty's Government would put no obstacle in their way'. To make the position even more firm he said that 'the current status of an independent Sudan under the Condominium Agreement of 1899 with Great Britain would remain'.

My role in all this was to listen to the skilful responses of Arthur Kellas, my fellow Embassy spokesman, at the daily press conferences. He was later to have a serious problem in making a statement after the coup d'état by Nasser, but, blissfully at this time, the British response in London and Cairo was robust and we were succeeding in holding our own against the barrage of propaganda. However, when Herbert Morrison, the Foreign Secretary, caused the despatch of the 1st Battalion of the South Lancashire Regiment to Khartoum to uphold that position, I was back in the seat as the Military Spokesman.

It then became a challenge for correspondents to write their despatches under Serag el Din's watchful determination to hold up, using Cable and Wireless, any reports critical of Egypt. This then became a balancing act, getting a cable through the censor or using my clandestine route which could rebound both on me and the correspondent. It is rare for 'spokesmen' and journalists to collaborate, but for the latter this was the only way to keep up the flow of unhindered news reporting and most used it. Another trick Serag el Din introduced was to get the clerks in Cable and Wireless to accept the copy as written with a 'black' (carbon copy), returning the latter as if uncensored, then deleting the Arab newspaper sources before sending it on; the Foreign Desk of any paper concerned was given the impression that a local canard was the considered judgement of a trusted correspondent. This became so unacceptable that some correspondents took the road to GHQ from where they could send unfettered background copy back for leader writers and diplomatic commentators in Fleet Street. Some papers, notably the *Daily Telegraph*, played it both ways by sending another correspondent to Cairo while Colin Read, their most experienced foreign correspondent, stationed himself at GHQ. Fearful of being 'scooped' by his colleague in Cairo, he would get up at 5.00 a.m. in the Canal Zone, dash to meet the Cairo–Ismailia night train and take the Cairo overnight papers from the Engine Driver, with whom he had made a financial deal. A fluent Arabic reader, he then 'milked the copy', double checked against our PR at GHQ and filed straight to London through the Royal Signal's set up, thus scooping the Cairo based press. This was to get me into trouble later when the replacement for Colin Reid in Cairo made an official complaint through the editor of the *Daily Telegraph* to the War Office saying that I was favouring Colin over him by giving Colin 'scoops'. When I told Colin he said 'Oh he is just a fourth floor man, ignore him'; I never discovered what that meant in *Daily Telegraph* jargon but I could guess.

I became well aware of the intense competition between newspapers and between the wire services from my previous experience with the press in East Africa and Mogadishu, where I had first met Colin Reid covering the border dispute between Somalia and Eritrea. I had not realised quite how acute this could be until I had a protest from the main press agencies in Cairo that I was favouring one over another by always telephoning Reuters first. So now I had to keep a daily roster and telephone Reuters, Associated Press, Agence France Presse, the Press Association and the Exchange Telegraph, rotating the batting order every day. A newcomer to this arrangement was Deutschen Presse-Agentur led by an impressive Dr Hans Rahm who he wanted to be first every day. A gentle reminder of the recent conflict between our two countries and the outcome was accepted with good humour and all continued to go well. In the end 'Soc' of Associated Press summed it up: 'Hey, I don't like being two minutes behind Haigh at Reuters, neither does New York.' A lesson I never forgot.

When the 16th Independent Parachute Brigade was flown from
Britain to the Canal Zone on 18 October 1951, the British Government
was only ten days away from a General Election. There was political
and military tension building up both in Cairo and London. Military
observers and the old Cairo hands would not be unaware that the
Gezira Sporting Club, strategically placed on Gezira Island and close
to the predominantly European quarter of Zamalek, had a racecourse,
golf course and open ground making it an ideal dropping zone for
this Brigade. I was always asked 'were there plans for such a drop,'
but avoided answering. In the meantime, the outposts of the army in
the Zone were increasingly being subjected to hit and run attacks by
Wafd inspired guerrillas in Ismailia and Tel el Kabir, with the British
garrison dependent on food supplies through these towns. My press
entourage grew by the day as the threat of military action to prevent
attacks on troops in these towns attracted more and more coverage.
The move of the Parachute Brigade was complete by October 20 and
included the 33rd Airborne Light Regiment.

But I was also living in two worlds. One was the ever busy offices of
the Information Office, with telephones ringing and correspondents
coming and going to and from many different countries; the other,
away from all this, was being led by the Cairo cosmopolitan elite *inter
alia* at the Gezira Sporting Club, Shepheard's Hotel and the Groppsi's
Tea Rooms, no doubt where Muhammad Fayed, the present owner
of Harrods, went as a small boy to have treats in his childhood.
The roof garden of the Semiramis Hotel was another spot where
one could dance until the small hours, cooled by a breeze from the
Nile and safe, one thought, in Garden City with the British Embassy
and other well protected residences. Or one could watch the British
Ambassador with quintessential calm playing golf at the Gezira Club,
often with one of the Military Attachés. My wife often swam with
friends in its enormous pool while the children played in the small
children's pool. In the midst of a bustling cosmopolitan city, this
was an oasis reflecting the Napoleonic charm of French boulevards,
squares and trees, and the appeal of surrounding restaurants, bars
and cafes. I would feel the same atmosphere in years to come when
posted to Paris. Even the legendary 'concierge' was replicated by a
'Boab' who slept, I am ashamed to say, on the floor of the entrance to
our block of apartments. I was to discover later to my cost that, as in

France, there was a close link between Boabs and the police, the one reporting to the other on the comings and goings of the occupants.

The cocktail parties and dinners went on. To find oneself eating off one's own plates and using well recognised knives and forks, or even glasses, at a host's table was a common occurrence. Often, guests who came for cocktails would not leave and stayed on uninvited to a pre-arranged dinner party – it never fazed a suffragi. If there was then a shortage of cutlery or anything else, even food, the suffragi's friends who had no 'masters' at home that night would rush from apartment to apartment through the darkened streets of Zamalek carrying whatever was wanted. Guests were rarely aware of what was going on. This was a free and easy style of entertaining which suited my press friends down to the ground. They could go or stay as the news dictated. And who would want to stop Ward Price, the legendary correspondent of the *Daily Mail*, recounting how he bought vintage French wine from the PX stores in Japan when he found a container sitting on the dockside listing rare and largely unknown vintages. On enquiring from the American officer in charge how this came about, it transpired that their buyers in France were given a map reference and told to buy everything in their allotted 'square' regardless of vintage or cost. The thought of these bottles being swilled down with a dash of coke to give an American flavour was sufficient excuse for Ward Price to buy, sight unseen, anything he could get.

But the lulls were few and far between in the build-up of tension by the Egyptian press and international concern over the security of the Suez Canal. The French Government made a statement on 20 October giving full support to the actions of the British Government, urging no withdrawal under pressure.[4] Emboldened by international support, the British Ambassador issued a statement holding the Egyptian Government responsible for allowing any 'disorders' in the Canal Zone. This had some effect as the Egyptian police started taking action in the Canal Zone and Alexandria where there had been further rioting and anti-British hysteria, resulting in the death of a civilian and four wounded. This was to have an unfortunate outcome in the Canal Zone, bringing the Egyptian police into conflict with the British garrisons in Ismailia and Tel el Kebir. Port Said was also targeted by the Moslem Brotherhood, inspiring local action against British troops working in the dock areas. A fatigue party of the Lincolnshire

Regiment was fired on, luckily without causing casualties. In the face of the these increasingly militant actions, Hastings Aircraft of the Royal Air Force Transport Command, flew in 3,000 men of the 19th Infantry Brigade. The 16th Parachute Brigade was at hand to cover their arrival and had taken up strategic positions.

CHAPTER FOUR

Flight from Egypt

I felt my own position and that of my family was becoming more dangerous and, without 'papers', vulnerable in the face of the anti-British atmosphere in Cairo. Each day I travelled from Zamalek in an army car, which had been allotted to me as a Lieutenant-Colonel and Assistant Director of Public Relations in the Canal Zone. A sturdy 'Vanguard' out of the Humber stable painted khaki, it had already attracted the attention of small boys throwing the inevitable stones. One day the engine made a rather horrible noise. I discovered that, while my faithful Sudanese driver, Tantawi, had been distracted, the local garage hand had dropped ball bearings down the dipstick hole. That cost the army £E30. My pleadings to the Command Secretary at GHQ, representing the Treasury, that he should pay for it to be painted any other colour but khaki fell on deaf ears. Tantawi fended off the urchins who threw stones, but I knew that with the deteriorating situation it could only get worse. Coming over the Kasr el Nil bridge each day before being able to reach Garden City, the protected enclave, I had to pass the old Victorian rose tinted brick barracks, which once would have held a British regiment but were now empty. One day a vision of white, which anywhere else might have been frost, covered the roofs and upper walls. As I slowed down, it revealed maybe a hundred or more 'fellahin' clad in their white galabiyya, the long simple robes of the Egyptian. They were attacking the barracks with great enthusiasm but with painfully useless tools. Their frustration in making little impression on the solid English brick and cement spilt over to me in my British army car; it was a race between being seen coming onto the bridge at one end and reaching the other before they could get off the barracks to throw bricks, courtesy of the British army.

There was also the problem that neither I nor my family had diplomatic cover as we should have left with all the British Service personnel shortly after the abrogation of the 1936 Treaty. How long it would take for the police to check my forged Embassy pass, which alleged I was a diplomat, in the event of being stopped and searched, was a matter of speculation. I doubted that the Embassy would look forward to discussing it with the Ministry responsible for receiving and holding the passports of diplomats and returning in exchange 'La Carte d'Identité', stamped as issued by the 'Ministère des Affaires L'Etrangère'. I was not to get a genuine document until I came back to Cairo as a fully fledged Military Attaché.

I was not surprised, therefore, to be contacted by 'Sammy' Sansom, a first Secretary of the Embassy. He had been an experienced wartime officer, with the rank of Major in the security service in Cairo, and was a linguist with a particular mastery of Arab dialects, having grown up in Cairo. I knew little about him at the time apart from his title, but I was later to learn that I could not have been in better hands; he had been the man who had managed to get Donald Maclean out of Cairo, claiming diplomatic immunity.[1]

In May 1950, Maclean, the Embassy's Head of Chancery, was arrested by the Egyptian police. The facts surrounding his arrest have since been released by MI5/6 and published in Christopher Andrew's book, *Defence of the Realm* (Crown Copyright Penguin, 2009). He writes that one evening, 'Maclean, in a drunken rage, had vandalised the flat of two female members of the US Embassy.' According to the press he was found later with a 'companion', both drunk, causing havoc aboard a Nile pleasure boat. The Egyptian police arrested him for his behaviour, resulting in Sammy's intervention. Andrew confirms that, at the time, no one, least of all the Foreign Office or MI5/6, had the slightest suspicion that Maclean was one of the 'gang of five' traitors recruited during their Cambridge days. The reaction

Above left and right: The cover of the Carte d'Identité.

The official inside of the Carte d'Identité, issued in exchange for the passports of diplomats.

in London when they got him back was merely to send him to a Harley Street psychiatrist.

Maclean eventually escaped to Russia in 1951, accompanied by Anthony Burgess, on Russian orders passed on by Sir Christopher Blunt, one of the 'five' still at large. The escape was simple. He left his flat in London on 25 May carrying a large cardboard box and boarded the 6.10 p.m. train at Victoria station. As Andrew concludes, 'the London Residency (the Russian minders) knew from studying the watcher's working pattern that they clocked off each evening and stopped work for the weekend on Saturdays at lunch time, with no Sunday working.' Sammy, thankfully, was a little more reliable, and although he had inadvertently played a part in helping a spy, he had nonetheless proved himself as a very capable 'fixer' in Cairo.

Back in Egypt, my exposure through using the civilian telephone exchange in Cairo to get through to Ismailia and connect up with the garrison switchboard continued, but there was no other way to get quick rebuttals from GHQ to the increasingly vicious coverage of *El Misr* and *Al Ahram*. Nor were these the only papers publishing a fantasy of heroic deeds against the army in the Canal Zone and, in particular, absurd stories of the GOC General Erskine; the favourite being that he was found disporting himself in various unlikely locations, including a nearby lake, with even more unlikely female companions. All had to be denied before some lately arrived reporter fell into the censorship trap of sending off a story quoting these local papers believing the 'story' would arrive at his newspaper in the form he sent it. My voice too was becoming well known. Sometimes when the line went dead for a day or more, not an infrequent occurrence in most Middle East exchanges, I would use the '22 army' wireless and talk direct to my contact at GHQ. Anyone in the Ministry of the Interior who might tune into that wave length could hear the conversation. The only safeguard was that often they would not hear the incoming voice transmission. As I was quoting anti-British stories from the local press, perhaps they might have thought I was a friendly foreign newspaper. However, it was not through any of my press activities that I was so very nearly caught. As the sole British army officer still in Cairo, except for the two Military Attachés with diplomatic cover, the worst interpretation would have been that I was a spy, and that could have put me in prison. I hate to think of what the fate of my wife and children would have been.

In the end, what alerted the Egyptian police was one of those unforeseen circumstances. A friend of my wife, recently widowed, came out to Cairo to stay with us before the abrogation days. I had had to sponsor her by visiting the passport office and giving my rank, position and address. So she had been given a visitor's visa but it had run out. Not wanting to bother me during the crisis, she had gone by herself to renew it. Not unreasonably, the Egyptian officer concerned asked where, as the sponsor, I was now living. Nothing happened immediately, but as October turned to November and my daily press conferences and communiqués had almost become routine, I thought I was in the clear, but then my telephone rang. It was just before the time I usually left my office and went home for lunch.

My wife, Jean, whom I had married early in the war, had served with the London Ambulances during the Blitz. One morning, having swapped her shift the previous night, she arrived at her digs in her ambulance station in Bayswater to find her bedroom hanging off the side of the house, sliced in half by a bomb. In Egypt some years later her voice was quite calm as usual: 'Darling, the police have just called at the front door asking for you. I shut the door in their faces and chained it. They seem to have gone.' I discovered later that the door had been opened by my nine-year-old daughter, Vivien, who was working on her stamp collection in the cloakroom by the front entrance. She saw three large men standing on our landing, but was immediately told to shut the door by her mother standing behind her. I phoned Sammy and told him what had happened. 'Go back, collect your wife and the children and rush to the Gezira Club. No arguments,' he said. Well, I thought, he must know that the Egyptian police would be as unlikely to cross the threshold of the Gezira Club as a wife would have been in trying to get into a club in England using the wrong door. After packing up the bare essentials, including most importantly two teddy bears, Tantawi drove us there us at breakneck speed. We stayed until further instructions were on the way. No police came. It could have been our friend's application to the visa office which sparked the enquiry about me or, more dangerous, that I had finally been identified as a British army officer in Cairo, or, indeed, a combination of both. Sammy was taking no chances and we spent that night in the home of the Head of the British Council. I did not enquire too closely why he seemed to accept this imposition at short notice, but I surmised that Sammy and he were not unknown to each other or to clandestine activities. I was just thankful for a refuge.

We were not to stay long. The plan was that early the next morning, certainly by six o'clock, we should be on our way to Heliopolis, the sealed border between the Cairo suburbs and the desert road to the Canal Zone. I was to drive an ancient Daimler provided by the Embassy. I presume the transport officer did not want to lose a better car. Sammy was to lead in his official Embassy car. So at the early hour we bundled the children into the back with their Teddy Bears and the suitcases and set off. Driving the Daimler for the first time I experimented with the self select gears mounted beside the steering wheel, while keeping an anxious eye on Sammy's car in front. To shift the gears up or down required first selecting the lever and then double declutching, whereupon, theoretically, the clutch engaged the right gear. Sammy's instructions were to follow him as closely as I could when we approached the barrier manned at that time of the morning, as he said, by a sleepy soldier. Sammy would present his correct documentation. The sentry would lift the barrier. Before he could lower it, encumbered no doubt by a heavy British Lee Enfield .303 rifle, I was to speed the car under the raised barrier and make a dash for the open road. It was unlikely, he said, that any car would be standing by, and within a few minutes we would be out of sight. He had not reckoned on my trying to hurry up the ancient technology. As I rushed to go up from first to second, nothing happened. No matter what I did the wretched lever would not engage the clutch. Slowly we ran, luckily downhill while the sentry I could see in my rear mirror was aiming his rifle to have a pot shot. What to do stop and give up, or try all of us, to get into Sammy's car which, by then was well ahead of me. At that moment I spotted a burnt out oil tanker on the side of the road, behind which I ran the car in neutral until I was partially hidden. By this time, I was far enough ahead for the sentry to wonder where I had gone and it would take time if he pursued on foot, an unlikely effort at that time in the morning. I leapt out, whipped open the bonnet and just banged about finding the strange lever mechanism on top of the engine casing. Back in the car I started up and tried again. We were off and up through the gears. I never found out what was wrong but guessed it was just my panic in fouling up the delicate sequence some Daimler boffin had invented.

There is also a road to the Canal Zone through Ismailia and the garrison town of Moascar, but that runs through small Egyptian towns and two cars with diplomatic plates would have attracted attention. Wisely, Sammy had chosen the desert road. The children in the back with their teddy bears seemed unfazed as we drove deeper into the desert. This would be the road the army would use if it was called upon to re-enter Cairo. That morning we had it to ourselves. There is something calming about the desert, and beautiful. The sun was rising behind us casting long shadows, but nothing to frighten us.

We kept a steady pace and the old Daimler purred as though to say I am making up for giving you the fright of your life at the barrier. The sun climbed higher and the lovely early morning of the desert turned to the sandy flat landscape one longs to leave. Eventually we reached GHQ for a late lunch and met old friends including Colonel 'Jock' Carroll whom I had fought with in Burma when he commanded, for a short time, a battalion of the Royal Norfolk Regiment. He was now Director of Public Relations for the army in the Middle East. Plans were discussed for our onward move to Nicosia in Cyprus, where I was told a King's Messenger would arrive with passports for myself, my wife and children, with stamped diplomatic visas showing that I had been appointed as a new Military Attaché arriving from the UK via Cyprus to join the British Embassy in Cairo. I was to bluff my way back from Cyprus by using civil aircraft. But then, lunching in the HQ Mess, I decided to enjoy a few days off with my wife and family.

My next means of transport was to be an RAF Transport Command *Valleta*, standing by at Fayid, the RAF base for the Canal Zone, ready to fly us to Nicosia, the capital of Cyprus. I did not think this could be just for me and the family as I was only too aware of peace time financial restrictions, but when we boarded on 25 November 1951 we had had only two days off and seemed to be the only passengers. I had been used to flying in Dakotas which had been so much a part of the Burma campaign, carrying out wounded and parachuting in supplies, or adapted for carrying thirty or more passengers. This looked a much more manoeuvrable plane which I had not encountered before, with limited room for passengers. We were soon to find out. Half way across the Mediterranean, the pilot received a message to look for a downed plane along his route. Suddenly, instead of relaxing to that high thrum of an engine which induces delightful drowsiness, we were dropping like a stone to sea level. Then up again and down again. My wife had started with a cold and rapidly developed sinus trouble. This was the first time my daughters had flown so they just thought it quite normal although Vivien, who had contracted amoebic dysentery from drinking unboiled water while in the Canal Zone, was violently sick and had to be rescued by one of the RAF sergeants travelling with us. We never spotted the plane so we righted ourselves and landed lightly, as one expected from the RAF.

We were glad to enter to the front of the Ledra Palace Hotel, the agreed rendezvous with the King's Messenger, and once again it all became an adventure for the young and a worry for the future for my wife and me. And where was the elusive King's Messenger? Nowhere to be seen. In those days carrying diplomatic bags round the British Embassies based in the cities of a far flung Colonial Empire was a job given to serving officers. Given two first class seats, one for the bags and one for the Messenger, many of us thought this a pretty soft touch and they could certainly arrive on time could they not? We waited three days before a message was left at reception that there was someone to see us in the bar. Well why not, and there he was wearing the obligatory blazer and flannels of an officer in muftis.

When he slipped me the passports between one drink and another and I glanced at them, I realised what a splendid job the Foreign Office had done and the timing had been better than one could have hoped. The date of issue by the Foreign Office was 13 November 1951 and they had managed to get the Egyptian Embassy in London to sign off the visas on the 23rd, leaving just two days while I was motoring to the Canal Zone and flying to Cyprus and the King's Messenger was *en route* from London. I had to say they were either genuine or the best forgeries one could have had. Most probably the former; why should the Cairo Embassy not have three Military Attachés when all the others only had two? I used them subsequently as the family passports travelling back to Cyprus on holiday from Cairo, and after a three year posting at the War Office on my way to SHAPE, outside Paris, in 1956. When I was stopped at Dover for the first time and asked where I had got my passport I thought it was clear enough, issued by the Foreign Office. 'Ah', but Customs man said, 'You haven't signed it'. Nor had I ever filled in a form which in those days required a signature on a stiff bit of paper which then peeled off at the passport office and stuck in the passport itself. At the Ledra Palace, between drinks, this passed us by.

Now there came the problem of getting back into Egypt. There was a local airport run by Cyprus Airways Ltd from which the Egyptian Airline 'Misr Air' flew to Cairo via Port Said, where one disembarked and went through immigration and customs.

We took off at two o'clock, determined to come back to Cyprus for holiday, having really enjoyed the few days away from the tension in Cairo and, indeed, the danger. But I reminded myself I was now a Military Attaché with diplomatic immunity, or so I hoped. I was near to losing it at Port Said. The questioning by a uniformed Egyptian officer was detailed. Had I been to Cairo or anywhere in Egypt previously? I was holding the hand of my elder daughter, a serious girl later to be ordained as a Deaconess. No, I said with a straight face, only to hear a small voice saying, 'but Daddy we have got a

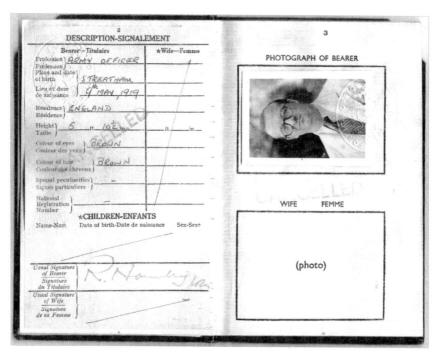

Inside of the author's passport handed over by the King's Messenger in Cyprus in November 1951.

flat in Cairo'. White lies are a bit sophisticated for nine year olds. Luckily this was not overheard or was ignored. So, our passports having passed inspection, and breathing a thank you to someone in the FO who had been really efficient, we embarked for the last stage, the flight to Cairo still with Egyptian Airlines. We were met once again by Sammy and re-united with my wife's friend who had kept the flat safe while we had been away.

My first question on getting back to the Embassy Office was to ask 'where were Tantawi and the army car?' Losing army equipment usually means paying for the replacement – in most cases a bit of webbing or a pair of boots, certainly not, I hoped, for a car. But knowing the Treasury, anything was possible. It had still been khaki when I left, which I had already told everyone was asking for trouble. I was quickly proved right. It had disappeared. But I did find a distressed Tantawi, who came shyly to my apartment the next day. 'They have taken it' he said. 'Who were they?' However, I was now a diplomat and I realised it was the duty of the police to protect me and my belongings. So a call to their HQ was the next step. I omitted to say that when I last used the car I should not have been in Cairo, but now I used my rank and name. It was a measure of the times that, while anti-British slogans were being printed every day by the press, I was treated with great courtesy as though nothing had happened since Nahas Pasha and the abrogation. What is more, a smiling Tantawi turned up a few days later with the car. At least he seemed happy that it was my car; it was now bright blue having had a quick Cairo style re-spray. I asked him where it had been and was met by a stony silence. Ismailia, it transpired, was where it had been, I suppose in its original army khaki colour and used for raids on the garrison. I was never to find out. Only, as always, the Treasury had won by getting the painting done for free.

CHAPTER FIVE

The British Army Responds

The War Office, as it was then, had not been idle in the short time I was away from the daily news situation. Over 5,000 troops had embarked on two of the Royal Navy aircraft carriers, HMS *Triumph* and *Illustrious*, bound for the Middle East. These were the days of ample reserves of troops to meet crises anywhere British interests were threatened, without, as today in Iraq, calling on the Territorial Army. The troops included the 1st Battalions of the Royal Enniskillen Fusiliers, 'the Buffs', and the Border Regiment, reinforcing the 3rd Division. While they started their sea voyage, the RAF had been busy. A further 6,000 soldiers had been air lifted to the Canal Zone from Tripoli, including the HQ of the 1st Infantry Division and the 3rd Battalions of two Regiments of Guards. From North Africa came the Cameron Highlanders. The RAF had flown 500,000 miles to move these troops and, in addition, had landed 170 tons of stores and 300 vehicles and guns. In the midst of these moves the 1st Battalion of the East Lancashire Regiment, which had been despatched to bolster confidence among the Sudanese who were under Nahas Pasha's threat of Egyptian sovereignty, were relieved by their sister Battalion, the South Lancashires. There was to be no homecoming, however, for the East Lancashires; they embarked at Port Sudan for Fayid, adding to the massive move of troops into the Canal Zone.

Nor had the world press been far behind. My press corps in Cairo was now building up on a more or less permanent basis. This was except for 'visiting firemen' expecting to file a few hours after arrival with only translations of local Arabic papers to hand – that is if they failed to touch base with the regulars who might have warned them that their first despatch could be denied before it arrived on their foreign news desk. Agence France Presse now had five correspondents using its offices with Jacques Marcuse and Ethel Thompson also covering for *Daily Mirror* 'exclusives'. The Arab News Agency, headed by Tom Little, had added two correspondents, Fred Gillett and Bill Holmes. Even the Japanese paper *ASAHI*, published in Tokyo, had sent a correspondent who I got to know quite well after the initial impulse to jump at him over my desk. He was the first live 'Jap' I had seen since coming out of Burma in 1946.

I slipped back into the routine of tracking down the ever more lurid stories of British troops' atrocities, and being attacked and outnumbered by the 'liberation militia'. At Zagazig, a small town some fifty miles west of Ismailia, it was reported in headlines by the local paper *Shaah Al Gadid* that wheat supplies for Tel el Kabir, where there was a major concentration of British forces, had been confiscated. At the time the British forces were building up, eventually to reach a total not far off 100,000 throughout the Canal Zone, from Fayid running down to Suez. Yet, surprisingly enough, there were still Egyptian army liaison officers at the Command HQ. Much later, after the coup d'état by Nasser, I was to meet and become friends with Colonel Anwar Sadat, our two families meeting together on occasions. I realised then the bond which exists between soldiers, even on opposite sides. Muhammad Neguib, first President of Egypt, proudly showed me his card at the first reception in Cairo after the coup. This bore the magic words for any British officer – PSC – Passed Staff College.

But all that was still to come. The stand-off between the two Governments remained and, indeed, was being underlined by statements from both. On 7 November the Conservative British Government had made clear, in no uncertain terms, its intention of maintaining their treaty rights. A long note delivered by Sir Ralph Stevenson, the British Ambassador, underlined the illegality of the actions of the Egyptian Government. He declared the abrogation to be contrary to the principles of the United Nations set out in paragraph three of the Charter, but at the same time he held out an olive branch to negotiate under procedures set out in the articles of the Treaty. Proposals for a Middle East Command, in which Egypt would have had full military participation, had already been rejected. They were rejected again a week later when 'National Struggle Day' was announced to mark the anniversary of 1918, when the then Prime Minister, Zaghlul Pasha, had first asked for independence.

In the midst of the celebrations and party leaders visiting the tomb of Zaghlul, the government suddenly called on the Egyptian press to curtail their inflammatory and baseless stories. If this brought temporary relief to the Embassy it was short lived. The Wafd press, seizing on the press reports of the proposed Middle East Command which invited Egyptian participation, sarcastically remarked that Egypt was already under occupation so how could she act freely? The claim that this was to face the Russian threat to the Middle East was described as 'a fabricated nightmare'.[1] The Western Powers were then accused of their 'Black Record' with America, causing the displacement of a million Palestinian Arabs. The danger was from Israel not Russia, the press 'leaders' ranted on, and was not Egypt already a member of the United Nations, dedicated to defend against aggression?

The seeds were being sewn for the approval of an armed conflict between Egypt and Israel but my press corps was being even-handed in their reporting, also giving coverage to the Wafdist press, much to the consternation of the Information Departments of the Embassy and the Foreign Office in London. The only recourse I had was to stick to the facts over the Canal Zone situation and daily, sometimes immediately, rebut the worst of the stories, leaving the diplomatic storm to blow itself out. But the Egyptian press, urged on by the Government, was having its effect on the local labour force employed by the forces. Random attacks from their fellow Egyptians increased, and in the face of this intimidation many began to leave their employment in the Canal Zone, including those working for service families. The RAF was forced to air lift a draft of 2,000 men from the United Kingdom to replace the Egyptian civilians employed in specialist trades on the base. Evacuation for service families was offered on the returning empty planes. The whole operation was accomplished in ten days, using the RAF Lyneham base.

In Cairo, the Christmas season started badly for the British. On 4 December, two soldiers were wounded in a flare up of fighting in Suez while driving through the town. Returning fire, which they were entitled to do under the rules of engagement, two Egyptian policemen were killed and several were wounded. Two days before, the 1st Battalion of the Royal Sussex Regiment had been involved in a serious confrontation when police auxiliaries opened fire, resulting in the death of a British officer, two other ranks, and eight members of the British army's Pioneer Corps from Mauritius, numbering some 10,000 throughout the Canal Zone. The sniping by so-called 'Liberation Forces', which included anyone who could get hold of a gun, added to the danger. Brigadier Greenacre, then commanding the British garrison in Suez, confronted the Egyptian Governor demanding that measures should be taken to maintain law and order and disarm the Egyptian police. From reports I was getting from the correspondents who had gone to Suez it was the police who were responsible for attacking British forces while the Egyptian army stood back and let them take the brunt of casualties. This was confirmed in a note sent by the British Embassy to the Egyptian Foreign Ministry on 6 December 1951, protesting that the incidents at Suez on 3 and 4 December showed that 'lawless elements were out of control'. It went on to identify these as receiving active co-operation from the 'guard companies of the auxiliary police', known as the Boulac el Nizam. It accused mixed bands of auxiliary police and civilians of 'making deliberate and unprovoked attacks on British troops going about their normal duties.'[2]

As the police casualties mounted, resentment at the lassitude of their army in the struggle was to boil over. None of us sitting in Cairo in early December of 1951 foresaw the devastation which was eventually to come to Cairo as the police, despite these protests, continued to attack the British army in Ismailia and throughout the Canal Zone. Despite this provocation, Lieutenant-General Sir George Erskine, commanding all British troops in Egypt, was patient. He told the press that he did not look upon the incidents as affecting the validity of the agreement he had made and that it was the police who were responsible for maintaining order in the towns, not the army. His patience was to be sorely tried and would come to an end, but, at the time, we all breathed a sigh of relief in Cairo.

British troops on patrol in Ismailia. (*Mirrorpix*)

During this situation, Tom Sefton Delmer of the *Daily Express*, one of the legendary foreign correspondents of the time, marched into my office. He was a tall and imposing figure, exuding self-confidence and wearing what I could only describe as a blue and white butcher's apron made into a suit. 'Where is the action?' he demanded. I said that we had had some trouble in Suez but you had better hurry if you want to get a story. He left at once with a dismissive gesture when I said I would be holding a press conference shortly. That, I gathered, was for 'ordinary' correspondents – gossip was that his expenses were unlimited. As he left, he paused, turned and said, 'Where do I get a plane?' I had had a similar experience with Claire Hollingworth that same day. She was then writing for the *Economist*, although she had a remarkable reputation as a war correspondent during the desert war, mainly based on her ability to get what she wanted from the most senior generals, planes being her favourite choice. 'Could I get a plane to fly her to the Canal Zone?' Clearly neither Tom nor she were used to dealing with mere Lieutenant-Colonels who could not whip up a plane at short notice.

The actions of the police, both in Suez and Ismailia, had not been allowed to pass without formal protests, but the reluctance of the

Egyptian army at this stage to take aggressive action against the British army showed that the residual goodwill between soldiers remained, unless they received orders to the contrary. I was to reap that benefit when I later met Colonel Anwar Sadat, but that was not to be until after the coup d'état. The Egyptian Foreign Ministry, in the meantime, was not lying down under rebukes from the British Embassy. The note which came back spoke of 'massacres and criminal aggression'. As the Cairo foreign correspondents had by now become used to my immediate denials, the figures in the Egyptian note alleging twenty-eight dead on 3 December, including seven policemen, and seventy wounded were not accepted, nor were the alleged fifteen dead and twenty-nine wounded on the following day. But whether or not the propaganda campaign was being accepted by the international press, the Egyptian Government continued to play for high stakes. Immediately following the Suez incidents it was announced that an Egyptian Minister of State would 'command all liberation battalions'. £E100,000 was allotted for military training. To cut the liaison between the British Armed Forces and Egyptian officers, the acting Minister of War and Marine, Abdel Fattah Hassan Pasha, recalled all the military missions in the UK arranged through the Military Attaché in London, and the withdrawal of British personnel attachéd to Egyptian military units.

If that was not enough to keep the Cairo correspondents on their toes, General Erskine announced on the following day that British troops would bulldoze several Egyptian mud houses in Ismailia to open a new safe road through to the 'vital' Suez filtration plant. Nor was he going to wait for a week which the Egyptian authorities had asked for. Indeed the operation would take place the following morning and the 16th Parachute Brigade had been sent to Suez to see that the final stages of the road would be completed. The plan was to build a bridge over the Sweet Water canal avoiding areas where clashes in Suez had taken place. Scenting a good story, my correspondents demanded access to Suez. The attitude of the Director of Public Relations in the Canal Zone, to which I was also answerable, was 'to let the dog see the rabbit'. Provided we knew where everybody was there was little restriction. Moreover, within the military boundaries in the Canal Zone the press could use the facilities provided by the Royal Corps of Signals and file direct to the UK or worldwide.

General Erskine announced he would not put his troops in danger after the previous experience. He confirmed that the Egyptian authorities had been warned of these movements, but in the absence of a formal reply and guarantees with regard there being non-armed police he would start the operation. The announcement set the Cairo press alight. The press corps reported in detail and the story was carried as headlines in the British press and worldwide to a greater or lesser degree. My telephone line through Ismailia – Moascar burnt up. My early evening press conferences were packed. The Embassy spokesman sitting in with me had his hands full.

The reaction of the Egyptian Cabinet was swift. A resolution was passed to recall their Ambassador from London as a protest at the aggression of British forces in Suez. This was followed by a number of statements. New houses would be built to replace those destroyed. Legislation was tabled to enable Egyptian citizens to carry arms, admittedly after the Minister of the Interior had agreed, but they were given a time limit to do so. The technical staff of the Embassy in London would be withdrawn and re-located to Switzerland.

All this played into the hands of the extremists within the Moslem Brotherhood, the power base of the Prime Minister Nahas Pasha. The diplomatic fury carried with it the possibility that Sir Ralph Stevenson might also be recalled *en rappel* if the Egyptian threat materialised. The following day it was reported that the Egyptian cabinet had met for a further three hours and the press were warned to expect 'an important announcement at 11.30 in the morning'. Nothing happened but one Egyptian paper declared that a decision had been made which would automatically call for the British Ambassador to leave. Other papers thought the delay was hopeful. This proved to be the case when, later in the evening, the British Ambassador presented a note to Ibrahim Farag Pasha, the acting Foreign Minister, recounting the facts of the recent actions by British forces in Suez. It emphasised that the demolition of some houses and building of new roads had been carried out specifically to ease friction.

The situation was further diffused when reports from Paris, where the Egyptian Foreign Minister Serag el Din was residing, said he was ready to meet Mr Eden, the British Foreign Minister. The Foreign Office let it be known that they would welcome a renewal of contacts between ministers. But this statement did not suit the propaganda

programme being waged by Serag el Din and the Wafd press. The next
announcement was of the arrest and imprisonment of two Embassy
employees charged with encouraging locally employed workers to
return to the Canal Zone. Whatever the truth, a crowd had waylaid
them on their way home and were well rehearsed in what to shout
for the benefit of bystanders. After a visit by an Embassy official, it
was confirmed that the two employees had been manhandled and
showed signs of ill treatment.

To add to the turmoil, the Government then decided to allow
the 'free arming' of the Egyptian peoples in their struggle against
'aggression', with penalties for anyone co-operating with the British
forces in the Canal Zone. This was followed by an order stating that
the Gezira Sporting Club was to be closed for 'housing development',
to compensate for the homes destroyed by the British in Suez. While
not attracting wide attention, it certainly startled the Egyptian and
European members residing in Cairo. In his efforts to whip up further
anti-British propaganda, Nahas Pasha had overlooked the fact that
the King was a sponsor of the Gezira Club and not an infrequent
visitor himself. On the other hand, Sammy Sansom, in November
1951, had been well aware that it was exclusive enough to hide my
family in while he made the arrangements to get us out of Cairo and
into the safety of the Canal Zone.

The Gezira Club was vast by any standards, covering a substantial
part of Gezira Island itself. It had a race course, golf course, tennis
courts and, most popular of all, swimming pools for young and
old. The Clubhouse was luxurious. At times of tension, the British
Ambassador might be seen playing golf with the Military Attaché,
'Cuthy' Goulburn, which had the desired effect of calming members'
fears. Nahas Pasha's threats were seen by the international press
as a sop to the Moslem Brotherhood, who were calling for more
aggressive action.

In the meantime, the Embassy Information Department kept in close
touch with the British and foreign residents through the circulation
of a 'news sheet', often giving the facts of the situation on a daily
basis to counterbalance the outpourings of the Arabic papers. It was
significant that the two local employees, beaten up and then arrested,
were a translator and a clerk from this department of the Embassy.
The Embassy had only learnt of their arrest through the local press

and that they had required treatment in the Kasr el Aini hospital before being removed to the Citadel prison. In 'Foreign Office speak' it was a gross discourtesy that their situation had not been reported first to their employer. Needless to say, no apology came from the Egyptian Interior Ministry. While, as in this case, press attention centred on the situation in Cairo and to a lesser degree in Alexandria, the military situation in the Canal Zone continued to make the headlines. American press interest continued to build up with the arrival of Tom O'Neil of the *Baltimore Sun* and Duncan Rollo from *Atlantic Monthly*. Then, shortly afterwards, correspondents from the American Broadcasting Company, ABC, the Christian Science Monitor and the Cleveland Plain Dealer arrived. I knew nothing of them at that time, but Soc once more helped me to understand their politics and standing in the USA. As December 1951 was drawing to a close, militant activities also died down in Suez with the exception of the derailment of a military train which was clearly sabotaged. *The Times* reported that this had been reported in the local press three hours before it happened![3] British troops, however, were still being attacked in Ismailia. The Dragoon Guards had been fired on while patrolling the garrison base and returning fire killed two of the attackers. In Cairo, the Moslem Brotherhood kept up its pressure for more militant action. To appease them, Serag el Din at the Ministry of the Interior released sequestered property taken off them in 1948 when they assassinated Oned Nokrashi Pasha. They suddenly found their funds had received a boost equivalent to £E200,000 at 1951 values.

In the comparative calm of the week preceding Christmas, General Erskine took the unusual step of giving an interview to an Egyptian journalist who remained anonymous. During this he outlined the present situation as he saw it and, in doing so, entered for the first time into the realm of Middle East politics. The interview was not published immediately. Instead the Embassy approved the text and circulated it to the Cairo and Canal Zone press. It was comprehensive and held out an olive branch to the Nahas Government. Erskine said that it was his role to protect the military establishments in the Canal Zone under the terms of the 1936 Anglo-Egyptian Treaty, and he would prefer to do this peacefully as an ally of Egypt. While distancing himself from the political issue of a commander embracing the Middle East as a whole, he questioned whether this could be accomplished with Egypt. Egypt could remain neutral unless she had allied forces comparable with those required the last time her territory was threatened. Such forces, he said, could only be assembled with allies pointing out that Egypt stood at the cross roads of the Middle East. The forces in the desert campaign had been no less than four armoured divisions and twelve infantry battalions supported by a substantial Air Force and Navy. 'Things were now drifting in a most dangerous manner', the interview continued, drawing attention to the recent sequence of events; the rioting and looting requiring armed intervention. The withdrawal of labour serving the army in the Canal Zone was represented as a patriotic action, but was in fact due to intimidation. Attempts to make arrangements with the civil authorities had been sought to no avail as the recent incidents at Suez had shown. General Erskine concluded this significant interview by recalling the long association of the British with the Egyptian peoples and his reluctance to see this lapse into bitterness and recrimination: 'but I do not despair of finding some way to reconcile our differences'.[4]

Whatever the impact of General Erskine's appeal to reason, which might have reached the Egyptian press in Ismailia following the Embassy's distribution, it fell on deaf ears in Cairo. Within a few days some fifty undergraduates from Fuad el Awal University, having completed their guerrilla training, were reported to be on their way to the Canal Zone encouraged, it was said, by the academic staff. Christmas was now only a few days away but any hope for a few days of peace in Ismailia was quickly shattered. An RAF staff car was fired on in the curfew area of Quay Mohammed Alia of Ismailia, luckily with no casualties. An RAF ambulance carrying passengers to hospital from the garrison at Moascar was shot up, but, again, without casualties. To round up the festivities on Christmas Eve, a saloon car drove through a camp on the outskirts of Ismailia, firing at random from its side and back windows.

Away from Ismailia, Moascar, and Suez, the political moves in Cairo took new and significant changes. The first was the unexpected appointment, made by King Farouk, of Alfifi Pasha to Chief of the Royal Cabinet. A sixty-five-year-old Doctor of Medicine, he had spent part of his training in Dublin and was no stranger to revolutionary politics. He had already served as a minister in Government and, most importantly, as a previous Ambassador in London during the 1930s. His previous diplomatic experience clearly showed at his first press conference when he blandly declared that he had not been privy to the discussions between Egypt, America, and Britain. His appointment gave him direct access to the King which upset Nahas Pasha, but more so Serag el Din. To defend his position, he issued an immediate statement denying there was any hidden agenda by the King to force the resignation of the Government. There was further apprehension when the then current Ambassador to the Court of St James, one Fattah Amir, recalled by Farouk to give advice on foreign affairs, promptly called on Sir Ralph Stevenson at the British Embassy in Cairo before reporting to the Egyptian Foreign Minister. *The Times* reported these political moves with comment, giving equal coverage to both the Egyptian and British Embassy statements with the accuracy we had all come to rely upon.[5]

It was certainly a relief to me not to be quoted as the Military Spokesman, and to be able to let Roddy Parkes and his team dominate the press conferences. They also had responded to a proposal made by Nuri Pasha, the Prime Minister of Iraq, visiting London for the re-organisation of the Arab League in association with the Atlantic Pact, to guarantee the defence of the Middle East with economic and military aid from the West. This infuriated Nahas Pasha who responded immediately saying he was not 'interested in mediation', but the immediate and total evacuation of British forces in the Canal Zone and the unity of the Nile under the Egyptian Crown. Sensing the tension building up again, the press corps flocked back to our daily press briefings.

Then, to feed the press with more lurid propaganda, Nahas Pasha announced that a law had been drafted to inflict a fine of £E1,000 on anyone supplying food to the British forces, and two years imprisonment for any Egyptian working for the British anywhere. This was a direct threat to British Embassy local staff, as well as those still in employment in the Canal Zone. My driver Tantawi, although Sudanese, was at risk, as was my clerk, most certainly, who knew all about my clandestine telephone calls to GHQ in the Canal Zone, passing press copy for journalists who risked avoiding press censorship. I warned my clerk and Tantawi of the increased risk and closed down the telephone link, except for receiving information on events which I could use to issue denials and thus frustrate the propaganda campaign in Cairo. Then an Embassy employee received a letter from the Liberation Forces threatening death if he continued to work there. To round off the campaign, an Egyptian paper offered a reward of £E1,000 to anyone who killed General Erskine. At my press conference that day, the Embassy spokesman said this was an incitement to murder.

The political actions of the King also continued to dominate the news with the appointment of Afifi Pasha to the Royal Cabinet and the withdrawal of Abdel Fattia, the Egyptian Ambassador in London, to become Foreign Affairs Advisor. As these actions were being reported by the journalists speculating on the next moves, a short history lesson was given by Arthur Kellas, my opposite number from the Embassy. It came as a surprise to learn that in 1936, on the death of his father King Fuad, Farouk, a young boy of sixteen, had ascended to the throne and put forward Nahas Pasha to be Prime Minister in 1942. The appointment was made in unseen circumstances.

During the war, Cairo was the headquarters for the operations in the desert and the Middle East as a whole; the war impinged on every political move in the city. At the time, Nahas Pasha was considered to be friendly to the British and they influenced his appointment. However, Sir Miles Lampson, then British Ambassador, decided that Farouk might waver at the last moment and to make sure the appointment was made and would stick, the British army stationed in Cairo brought up armoured cars and surrounded Abdin Palace with Farouk inside. The long term effect of this threatening move was to cause resentment and humiliation in the Egyptian army whose duty it was to protect their King. This was brought home to me when I met Anwar Sadat and he said, 'You never treated our army with respect'. He had begun to form the Revolutionary Officers' Association as early as 1939. This action in Cairo was grist to the mill for his campaign against the British occupation, as he saw it, of his country, and the compliance of the King and senior officers of the army.

Although Farouk's sexual excesses and playboy life style were known to journalists writing society columns and by his own entourage and the 'high society' in which he moved outside Egypt, he had been respected and indeed loved by the Egyptian fellaheen as a young King. His peccadilloes, however, were well known by the revolutionary group of army officers. Their first action on seizing power, after Farouk's flight from Alexandria, was to put on display the contents of his very private collection of pornography. But that was to be in the future and, as with the press corps of all nationalities in Cairo at the time, I never risked making any offensive comment about Farouk personally. My own position was difficult enough as it was and retribution would have been swift.

So the reporting of one Arthur Cook of the *Daily Express* provided some light relief when he thought he had a scoop, no doubt fed to him by a local stringer, that a distinguished citizen of Cairo, Aboud Pasha, was gun running for the Moslem Brotherhood. Arthur always dressed in natty flannels and a blazer and had a reputation for scooping his rivals; his favourite way of getting behind a rival was to *Cherchez La Femme*. A pretty dangerous ploy in a Moslem community. But he got his story wrong about Aboud Pasha. Far from being a gun runner, Aboud was a highly respected and very rich member of the community. He promptly sued the *Express* group. Arthur left Cairo at speed for Tehran to cover the Persian oil crisis, the future for Prime Minister Moussadeck, the revolution, and the fall of the Shah of Persia, Britain's firm ally in the Middle East.

I only learnt of all this when my phone rang and another *Express* foreign correspondent, Tom Clayton, 'clocked in'. He invited me to dinner at the Semiramis Hotel, only half a mile from the Embassy. I thought I owed myself a 'freebie' as the War Office had failed to pay any expenses or living allowance at the time and hotels like the Semiramis were out of my league. Tom did me proud, immediately ordering a bottle of champagne. When the second arrived in due course I said, 'we all know the Beaver is generous about expenses with the likes of Sefton Delmer ordering planes or anything else to get story, but hardly entertaining a "spokesman", military though he may be.' 'Oh it's alright,' he said, 'it's all on legal expenses.' Then it dawned on me that all the questions about Arthur and Aboud Pasha were the reason for his sudden arrival to try and unseat the libel case. I could offer little help, but later I did put him in touch with Tom Little, the most experienced journalist in Cairo with a wide range of contacts. If anyone could help ease the situation it would be him. I departed well fed, expecting that would be the last of it, but Arthur Cook's name was to emerge again before long when the story of his assignment to Tehran went the rounds of the press corps, no doubt leaked by Tom. Apparently, when Moussadeck was condemned to be hanged following his trial after the debacle of the revolution, Arthur had shot his bolt by reporting it had already happened, when in fact he was a day early. He made up for it with a 'flash' the next day, only to have to 'kill it' when once again the hanging was delayed. His foreign news editor had had enough. His cable to Arthur simply read 'Either Moussadeck hangs tomorrow or you do.'

CHAPTER SIX

The Crisis Deepens and the Egyptian and British Casualties Mount

The camaraderie among foreign correspondents reflected the tension they all faced in covering on-going news stories and, at the same time, in never being 'late' with a story filed by the competition. The Metropolitan Hotel in Cairo was where they let their hair down with drinks all round after a wearisome day. Yet even then the most frequent questions to each other were 'have you filed yet?' This was the short hand for 'have you got a story I have missed'. The past master at evading this was Ralph Izzard of the *Daily Mail*, later to achieve fame by reaching base camp of the Everest expedition led by Sir John Hunt in an attempt to break *The Times* exclusive coverage of the attempt to reach the top. I met him the day he had slipped off to Suez and got an exclusive on the Italian oil tanker breaking the embargo on the shipment of oil to Israel by evading the port authorities. I am sure his answer to those drinking with him at the Metropole on whether he had 'filed' was to look blank and order another round of drinks. When Sefton Delmer left my office murmuring, 'leave me out of your open invitation for correspondents to visit the Canal Zone HQ, I'm off to Suez', he got the first story of casualties, among them were two British officers wounded and a soldier of the Buffs. This instinct was why he had unlimited funds given to him by Beaverbrook, the owner of the *Daily Express*, and he knew how to use them!

It was the first week of January 1952 and once again my telephone had been cut off somewhere along the line to Ismailia. I was relying on press and Embassy reports. Shots had been fired by snipers from civilian buildings close to roads north and south. These roads were used by British army contingents and were vital for supplies and communication. The response had been to deploy a troop of the 4th Royal Tank Regiment to 'take them out'. The result was devastating. Armed with 20 pounder shells the houses were reduced to rubble. I was asked about the use of this heavy weaponry. I was asked 'what is a 20 pounder?' The term had been used since and probably before Waterloo and denoted the weight of a round cannon ball to differentiate between heavy and light artillery, with light artillery firing a lighter ball. I was only too well aware of the difference as my regiment had suddenly been converted to an anti-tank regiment equipped with 4 pounder anti-tank guns. These were tiny two wheelers almost like large toys hoisted into the back of a canvas covered 'portee', a name meant to sound better than just a large truck. To go into action the portee would be driven towards the enemy tank, swiftly turned round and the gun let down from the back with a wire pulley, while the gunners scrambled round from the front seats and took aim at the enemy tank. Luckily I never saw action with one of these because it was soon realised that a 4 pounder, even with an armoured tip round, would fail to penetrate and explode inside the tank. Quickly abandoned, they were replaced by a tractor-drawn 6 pounder and later a 17 pounder, which then became the standard anti-tank gun for the remainder of the war. The deployment of this tank troop with, in this case, a 20 pounder gun, was a deliberate 'raising of the stakes', but ultimately the reason was to save the lives of British soldiers. The use of overwhelming force in the initial stages of dealing with riots has been a lesson sadly unlearnt in the later conflicts in the Middle East.

'Aid in support of the Civil Power', the term used to justify armed intervention in a civil conflict, is the most distasteful of duties an army can be called upon to carry out. I was lucky as here in Cairo in the early 1950s there were journalists who had been war correspondents during the recent war with Germany and Italy. They understood the role of an army and the problems soldiers faced in circumstances such as Suez, and reported accordingly. Among them was Alan Whicker,

A British road block in Ismailia, January 1952. (*Mirrorpix*)

the foreign correspondent for the Exchange Telegraph, a news agency in competition with Reuters. Alan had served the agency throughout the Italian campaign and shot to fame with his BBC series, 'Whicker's World', some thirty years later, followed by a brilliant series of TV reports on his war time experiences in Italy, being repeated in 2006. I felt I had played a small part in his very successful move to the BBC when he came into my office to say that the Exchange Telegraph was closing its foreign coverage and he was out of a job. Patrick Smith then walked in about something else, overheard Alan and said 'what about the BBC?' I was not to meet Alan again until 1960. When he asked me to appear on his BBC series, 'In Town Tonight', I had just retired from the army and taken up the position of press attaché to the Archbishop of Canterbury. My job was to head up an information office for the Church of England, the first ever attempt by the Church to deal professionally with the press, as I discovered when I asked to see their current press 'list'. It named only two papers, *The Times* and the *Church Times*. When I presented my first press release, naming all the press, I was told by Lambeth that it was not necessary as the papers took down the news from the BBC at six o'clock.

While the situation in Suez had been stabilised by the discipline and good soldiering of the 1st Battalion of the Royal Sussex Regiment, the situation at Ismailia had deteriorated badly. General Erskine had had to record a broadcast to call attention to the state of civilian anarchy. He said they were 'milling about the streets carrying tommy guns, terrifying the local population and in effect challenging the authority of the Egyptian Government.' Substitute guns for bombs and the picture will be familiar to readers today. Comparing the role of the police in Suez and Ismailia, he said they had behaved badly in both cases and encouraged rather than suppressed the rioting. Once again a situation to be repeated fifty years later with little learnt by the British Governments of the day.

There was a press centre based within the United Services Club itself, within the Moascar protected garrison, and only a few miles from the centre of Ismailia. The headlines in the British and worldwide press and on BBC world service reflected detailed coverage of the events. Some 1,200 troops were deployed in the region, but none in the town of Ismailia itself, giving little excuse for the outbreak of violence. But, although Ismailia caused concern, it was Suez that gave General Erskine the most difficult problem. With its water filtration plants and status as delivery point for all the oil supplies, a serious situation would arise if there was disruption, even for a short time – 'The economic life of Egypt would whither away', the General declared . I noted from my Cairo office that a 'Military Spokesman' asked to comment was reported in *The Times* as saying, 'It is doubtful whether the Egyptian police would be able to keep the armed civilian element in Suez under control.' A masterful understatement in the best military tradition.

Life for the British troops in the Canal Zone was also deteriorating as more Egyptian labour was withdrawn under threats from Serag el Din in Cairo. This base, the largest ever to have been maintained in peacetime outside the Indian sub continent, required an immense local labour force to support the military units, especially if it was to remain as a pivotal element of Middle East strategy. The buffer, at that time, between a civilian labour force and the army was the Mauritian Pioneer Corps. Ten thousand strong, their military role was to act in support of front line troops, not as civilian labour. They had a proud tradition. In Mauritius they were a respected as an elite body of men, many claiming European status arising from mixed marriages during the occupation of the island, first by the French and later the British who captured it during the Napoleonic wars to safeguard the sea route to India. Not for them was the labour on the sugar plantations. This had led inevitably to massive immigration from India in the colonial period. When I had been sent there in 1948 from Kenya to discuss increasing the recruiting for the Pioneer Corps, the Governor of the Island, Sir Bindon Blood, told me that already twenty-five languages were being spoken and the 'Indian' was no longer a labourer in the fields, but a provider of employment for the hitherto 'European' Mauritian. 'What we had now was all that we were going to get.'

The War Office had already turned to Cyprus and Malta to provide additional labour, but now, in the tradition of pre-war Empire, the African colonies under the jurisdiction of the Colonial Office came under review as an another source, and labour battalions were raised. General Erskine predicted that when these arrived, the base could be self-sufficient without local Egyptian labour support.

While Suez was experiencing comparative calm following the use of tanks to neutralise the sniping, Ismailia, even in the third week of

Armed British soldiers in a street in Ismailia, January 1952. (*Mirrorpix*)

January 1952, was still in turmoil. *The Times* summed it up in one paragraph: 'The "native" quarter of Ismailia bore all the appearance of a Town occupied in war'.[1]

GHQ had been forced to send in a battalion of the 16th Independent Parachute Brigade. Once again, as in the past, and would be so in the future, this formidable force, wearing the distinctive red beret, quickly dominated the situation on the ground. But again, with the strength of the forces at a commander's disposal, they were backed by Bren gun carriers and Centurion tanks. There was good reason for this show of force. By then an officer and two 'other ranks' had been killed. The American Convent had come under attack and Sister Anthony, an American national, had been killed. She was being buried in the Moascar garrison cemetery just as the forward elements of the para brigade were reaching the outskirts of Ismailia. Twelve terrorists had been captured the day before her burial, one on the very same morning hidden in a closed tomb. A request for a Moslem presence at the burial had been refused on the direct orders of Serag el Din. A Roman Catholic priest officiated and British civilians were present. A later search revealed a quantity of arms concealed in two Moslem tombs.

Some semblance of law and order eventually returned to Ismailia and a sullen but peaceful mood resulted. The presence of the police barracks on the outskirts of the town, however, had done nothing to bring this about. Senior officers may have wished to co-operate as professional policemen, but once again orders from Cairo were specific. The aggression against the 'occupying forces' was to continue and was a direct incitement to the militant extremists.

It was widely rumoured that a police 'Captain', trained at the Metropolitan Police staff college at Hendon, had been responsible for leading many of the attacks on British forces. General Erskine once again warned that he could no longer tolerate this unsatisfactory situation with the police failing even to attempt to maintain law and order or enforce curfews. He described the death of Sister Anthony as monstrous. A cordon was thrown round Ismailia and a house to house search made for the terrorists responsible. Suspected individuals were removed, but the elderly and infirm were omitted from the searches. While this gave some confidence to foreign nationals living there, many did not think it had come soon enough and there was no confidence in

Civilians under the watchful guard of British soldiers in Ismailia, January 1952. (*Mirrorpix*)

the Egyptian police force from those residents. Witnesses had confirmed that British troops had been shot at from the police barracks. This lack of control by senior officers of the police force denied the possibility of co-operation between them and senior officers of the army. Nor had the Egyptian army taken any direct action against British forces, and indeed a senior liaison officer was still at General Erskine's HQ. The Cairo riots, which were to come within a few days and lead to the partial destruction of the city, were to be the result of a contingent of the Ismailia police, marching on Cairo demanding that their army should be fighting the British with them.

Eleven men had been arrested and questioned as a result of the house searches, one being a well known secretary of a hard line group, but at the cost of the life of a para officer shot in the back. What was disturbing was that the fatal round came from a standard British army weapon, the universal sten gun. A further search of the tombs opened up a warren of vaults and graves to reveal a cache of 5,000 rounds of light bofor ammunition for anti-aircraft guns, which could also be used for ground attack, and more sten guns and bombs obviously assembled from the anti-aircraft ammunition. It was hoped this find would cripple the activities of the rogue elements of the police. It may have done so in Ismailia, but a document discovered at Tel el Kabir quickly doused any false hopes.

A direct order from Serag el Din to Lewa Mohammed Abdulla Raoul Bey, the Inspector General of Police, not to co-operate with British forces was found, threatening him with a Police Court Martial if he did not carry out Government orders to protect Tel el Kabir from British 'attacks'.[2] An operation was mounted to arrest him, together with some hundred police accused of firing on the British troops taking part in the recent search operations. In fact, he and the police under his direct command had already been released as there was insufficient evidence to link him with the shooting from the barracks in Ismailia.

On the diplomatic front, charges and counter charges on the death of Sister Anthony continued unabated. At the United Nations, a spokesman for the Egyptian Delegation made the astounding statement that her death was the result of a British plot to influence

Arms seized in Ismailia, January 1952. (*Mirrorpix*)

American public opinion. He quoted the bombardment of Alexandria by the British Navy as a precedent. Challenged on these statements with regard to the death of the nun he quoted the police HQ in Cairo. This was followed as usual by Serag el Din calling a press conference and sending two notes to General Erskine, relating to the events in Ismailia, saying the army had 'let loose savage dogs among unarmed people, crucified Egyptian civilians and desecrated Moslem tombs.'

Those members who were on the whole unsympathetic to the British action in Egypt knew full well by now that my early denials – direct to their foreign news editors via my Canal Zone link – might well arrive before their own copy. The pro-British press, while always fairly reporting both sides, tended not to repeat the more hysterical outpourings of the Egyptian Government. What would be unbelievable today to journalists reporting from countries overseas such as Iraq is what their colleagues had to do to file a story. In Cairo it meant getting to the one and only Cable and Wireless Office, handing in a top copy and getting a 'black' back with a receipt. These offices, although technically non-Governmental, were under the eye of the Ministry of the Interior. I later discovered that they put in censors as the crisis in Cairo worsened. The clever device was to accept and receipt the correspondent's copy and then alter the text by the simple means of deleting the source of the story if the journalist was quoting from an Arabic paper. So to the news editor in London, or wherever, it appeared to be an eye witness story from the writer, probably defaming British action. That this was frustrated in most cases was a tribute to sub-editors in reading between the lines, and their ability to check on the facts and denials, uncensored, sent by myself and my opposite number in the Canal Zone direct to the papers concerned using the Royal Corps of Signals

Frustrated by his failure to rouse the police into even more offensive action, and no doubt with the support of his Government, Serag el Din announced that now 'forcible action' would be taken directly against the British military garrison at Moascar. This was the first indication that military action might be taken against the British army, no doubt an unwelcome surprise to the Egyptian liaison officer still advising General Erskine at his HQ. Erskine's response, as usual, was quick and concentrated on protecting his soldiers' lives. A battery of twelve light anti-aircraft guns to be used in a ground role was deployed round the perimeter of the base. The right flank of the 3rd Infantry Brigade was reinforced and contained a small contingent of the Egyptian army! Later in the day, heavy Vicker's machine guns, used with such devastating effect in both world wars, were trained on government buildings, one of which contained the HQ of the police. Questioned by the press on the possibility of future military action involving the Egyptian army, Erskine gave the classic Army Chief reply, 'that would be a matter for my political masters.'

The war of words continued with a statement from Cairo that the operations in Ismailia had not lowered the morale of the Egyptian people: 'there was no room in Egypt for the British.' Ali Helma Bey, the sub-governor of Ismailia nearer the action than those in Cairo, made a conciliatory statement to the assembled press corps there, saying that he accepted it was his duty to expel the terrorists operating in the town, but that British military action had superseded his authority.

A Bren gun trained on a government building. (*Mirrorpix*)

CHAPTER SEVEN

Black Saturday, 26 January 1952

In Cairo, the Iraqi Ambassador was visiting Farag Pasha, the acting Foreign Minister. This led to immediate speculation that the visit might be a diplomatic intervention to try and seek some rapprochement between Egypt and Britain, bearing in mind that, at that time, Iraq had close and friendly ties to Britain. However, a statement from the British Embassy soon put paid to that notion by emphasising that under the 1936 Anglo-Egyptian Treaty, British forces had every right to be where they were. Reference was made to the visit only two weeks previously by Mr Anthony Eden, Britain's Foreign Minister, when he had made this clear to the Egyptian Government. What was not said officially, but confirmed by the Embassy spokesman sitting beside me, was that the dissident police officers responsible for the attacks in Ismailia and elsewhere had been urged on by the Moslem Brotherhood, to whom the Egyptian Government were in thrall.

These attacks continued as we sat in Cairo, and the next news from the Moascar garrison was to get headlines round the world; all the Cairo based journalists were besieging my office. General Erskine had delivered an ultimatum to the police HQ to stop the firing on British troops from the roof tops and windows of the police barracks. It was ignored. Two tanks were brought up to face the barracks. The firing continued and further warnings were broadcast. There was no response again. Forty rounds were then fired into the building. Forty-one police were killed immediately. Many, it was alleged later, were recruits. There was more to come as troops encircled a camp east of Ismailia to find a concealed Egyptian Armoured unit and, between Ismailia and Ryad, a small nearby town, a search identified six armed police who were wanted by intelligence and later admitted to previous attacks on the filtration plant at Suez. Once again I was faced with the dilemma of whether to open up my 'civilian' line through the exchange at Ismailia, who would put my civilian clerk through to the military exchange at Moascar, connecting to my office there with the facility to pass copy to London. The penalty if this was discovered, both for correspondents and myself, could be immediate expulsion from Egypt, even with my diplomatic cover. Up to now, correspondents had been very selective and cautious about when to use it. The decision to open it also had to be agreed by all those based in Cairo to avoid anyone taking advantage and getting a scoop behind the backs of their competitors.

Throughout the past months I had been guided by the Embassy Information Department, but above all by the long-term resident journalists. The doyen of these was Tom Little, manager of the Arab News Agency, who also wrote for *The Times*, the *Economist* and as a 'stringer' for several papers if a resident correspondent was away from Cairo. But Tom, with his extensive knowledge of Egyptian affairs, was a far more respected journalist than that latter term implies. He was to become a friend and gave me much wise advice without ever compromising his independence in what he reported. Another journalist who became well known internationally was Jan Morris, then reporting for *The Times*, who left Cairo to cover the successful Everest Expedition under Sir John Hunt. James Holburn for the *Glasgow Herald*, later to become its editor, was another I would be in touch with many years later while working at Lambeth Palace.

There was little doubt on the morning of 27 January 1952, the day following the shelling of the police barracks, that every means of communication was being demanded by the press corps. They were telling me that riots had started in Opera Square as a column of police, thought to be auxiliaries, marched on it shouting to the crowds assembling there and stirring them up. The press corps said it was not

A looted shopping centre on Fuad el Awal Street, Cairo, not far from the ruined Turf Club. (London Illustrated News, *9 February 1952*)

clear what they were shouting about, but then they reported that the leaders had spotted an Egyptian in uniform sitting on the outside balcony of the Badia Club, a favourite day time place for morning coffee, with a female companion. Whether the man was police or military was unclear, but he became the target for their grievances. Baying for blood, the nearest demonstrators rushed the steps up from the street, picked him up and threw him over the balcony railings. He did not survive according to some of the reports I was getting.

It was clear at that moment that the police contingent was directing its fury at the Cairo police and army for not attacking the

British in Ismailia as they had done, and been killed in their barracks. What happened then was not clear. I was busy telephoning the Canal Zone with early copy for several papers when reports from the Embassy warned that the demonstration had turned into a full scale riot with mobs shouting anti-British slogans. Members of the Moslem Brotherhood had been recognised organising it. Anwar Sadat, later to become President of Egypt, told me when we became friends after the coup d'état and abdication of Farouk that he had used the Brotherhood to attack the British army in Ismailia; their role in inciting anti-British action was well established.[1] Serag el Din was also known to have used the Moslem Brotherhood and it was surmised that on hearing the slogans being shouted as the police entered Opera Square, he quickly organised a 'rent-a-mob' to change the chants. It proved to be a dangerous move. By the end of the day nearly all the principal buildings in Cairo associated in any way with the European or British occupation had been burnt to the ground, and a pall of smoke hung over the city. 'Black Saturday' was the headline of the newspapers. It was ironic that the riot started within sight and sound of Shepheard's Hotel, the watering-hole of many of the American press who had started the day, if not applauding the demonstrators, in no doubt that the British were getting their come-uppance. By the afternoon the rioters had come back and burnt the hotel to the ground, causing those Americans still there to flee in whatever they 'stood up in' – in the case of two women who came straight to my office, not very much.

The offices of the British Overseas Airways Corporation (BOAC) and Barclays Bank were early targets. Then the cinemas, such as the Rivoli, which showed English films, were attacked – the English manager only escaped with his life by the help of his Greek staff. Well known restaurants and bars used by British residents and the press for meetings were next. Any place selling alcohol went up in flames, helped along by the bottles of spirits. In the midst of all this mayhem who should come into my office about midday but one of the oldest and most highly respected members of the Cairo British community. He was also a member of the Turf Club, one symbol more than any other that spelt 'British'. 'What about a drink and a spot of lunch at the Club?' he said. 'Surely you have heard about the riot in Opera Square?' I replied. His reply was symptomatic of the old Cairo hand,

'Oh we are used to those, it will die out very quickly.' Within the hour he had been hacked to death as he tried to fend off a mob attacking the entrance to the Turf Club. He had been dragged into the street, his corpse soaked in petrol, and set alight. The Canadian Trade Commissioner, a fellow member, suffered a similar fate. Having gained entry to the club, the mob chased members through the rooms, ransacking as they went from the top to bottom, setting everything alight. Burning was to become the hallmark of the rioters. The only defence weapon, I was told later by a correspondent who had managed to speak to a member, was a starting pistol.

Cairo was becoming increasingly enveloped in smoke and my personal concern was for news of the situation at Zamalek. This was the mainly European and middle class residential district where my wife, two children and my wife's friend visiting from England were, I hoped, locked in our flat. It was not far from the Gezira Club, of which Farouk was President, which I hoped would be a safe place once again if they had to flee, as we had done when we escaped from the police the previous year. My real fear was that the leaders of the riot would target the apartment blocks and light fires in the entrances with the draft of open doors propelling flames to the upper floors. Reports I was getting from the 'front' confirmed that this method had been used in city buildings now on fire. When eventually I got through on the phone, which was still working by a miracle, my wife said in her usual calm voice, 'it's alright, we are playing charades to keep the children from looking out of the windows'.

It was not, of course, only the resident British community which was at peril. The rioting terrified the Egyptian people sheltering in their homes when they realised that little or no effort was being made by the police to control it. Jehan Sadat, writing in her autobiography some thirty years later after the death of her husband, recalls the riots as a young girl of eighteen married to Anwar, a serving soldier who had telephoned from Farah where he was stationed, begging her not to go into the streets. Living with her parents at the time, she paints a vivid picture of what she was seeing. 'I rushed with my parents onto the roof to see clouds of black smoke and flames shooting up all over the city. What a horrid sight it was. It looked as if the whole country not just Cairo must be on fire.'[2] There is a poignant sentence as she hears on the radio that the Rivoli and Metric cinemas, 'where Anwar

A destroyed British Travel Agency in Cairo. (London Illustrated News, *9 February 1952*)

and I had often gone and the Jewish owned department stores where I had shopped for my trousseau,' have been burnt. As I was reading, by a strange co-incidence the BBC was running a programme on childhood memories. A contributor recalled her father arriving at their home blackened and distraught. His English bookshop had been burnt – 'it's all gone', she remembers him saying. Sadly he died within few days from a heart attack, one of the seventeen British and other Europeans to die as a result of that day.

Jehan must have spent all day on that roof for she continues with her eye witness account. 'Every business associated with a foreign presence was aflame. Ford's Automobile showrooms and Barclay's Bank burned. Liquor stores and the bars and restaurants, the St James's, the Cecil were all firebombed as well, the flames changing colour and growing even higher when the liquor bottles sitting on the shelves exploded. Last to burn,' she continues, 'was the world famous Shepheard's Hotel, which had once been the palace of a Turkish Bey. Anwar and I had never been there for it was too fancy and expensive for us, but the hotel had been a favourite haunt of British officers.'[3] Indeed it had been so when Cairo had been the 'rest and recreation centre' for Montgomery's desert army. Artemis Cooper, in her book, *Cairo in the War*, recalls that 'the stocks of decent Hock and Champagne did not run out until 1943. Even then there was no shortage of Algerian, Palestinian or South African wine'. Founded in 1841, now with its magnificent interior rooms, ballroom and 'long bar', not to mention the terrace where American journalists had been lounging at the start of the riot, the Shepheard's international reputation was equal to that of Raffles of Singapore. In no way could even the Cairo police ignore the fire alarm from there when they got it in the early afternoon of that awful day, and which was immediately picked up by the correspondents filing a stream of reports from my office. I was told there was little hope of saving the building. As the hose pipes were un-reeled by the fire brigade, they were cut by the rioters who had started the fire. The water was gushing into the street. Those American guests still sitting on the terrace, thinking the mobs had done with that part of Cairo after the morning 'show', rushed back to their rooms to salvage what they could. But the arsonists had started their fires at the back of the hotel where the rooms were and some were too late.

It was then approaching late afternoon and I was still relying on the press for the latest news as they asked me for comment or to use my facility. One of my best sources was Patrick Smith of the BBC who had contacts in the city and whose office was only a few doors away from mine. I was with him when my clerk rushed in saying 'please come quickly, there are two angry ladies in my office demanding to see you'. One I recognised at once as Margurite Higgins of the *New York Herald Tribune*, whose reputation for tough talking to anyone

All that was left of the famous Shepheard's Hotel after the riots of 26 January 1952. (London Illustrated News, *9 February 1952*)

who stood in her way had preceded her. Nor was the 'trib' very friendly towards the British; I had crossed swords with her once or twice already. Standing beside her was another lady, not a journalist as far as knew, wearing a long fur coat but, so far as I could judge, not much else. Both had fled from Shepheard's Hotel. As soon as I opened the door, Margurite Higgins said in a tone with which I was familiar, 'Why the Hell aren't the Brits doing something about the riots.' It was clear that they had lost everything except what they could grab as the fire reached their rooms. I was sorry but had to say I could do nothing and advised them to go the American Embassy which was within the same compound as my office and the safest place to be. It was not until many years later, when I read Max Rodenbeck's extensive history of Cairo, *Cairo City Victorious*, which touched on the events now taking place, that I discovered who the other lady in the fur coat was. According to Rodenbeck she was a Miss Christina Carroll, a soprano who was to have sung at the Cairo Opera House that evening.[4]

My curt reply at dealing with these two distressed ladies was to some extent excused by an urgent message to report at once to the Ambassador. Unknown to me, while the main body of rioters, having sacked the city, had gone down the Pyramid road with its tourist attractions of bars and restaurants, even Farouk's favourite casino,[5] a breakaway mob had turned onto the Kasr Nil Bridge, taking the road which led to the Semiramis Hotel, a prime target for looting and burning only 500 yards from the Embassy. As I entered the Ambassador's study I saw standing there the Military Attaché, Brigadier Goulburn, the Minister, the Ambassador's second in command, Head of Chancery and others. I had little doubt that we were facing a crisis. I had been aware of the contingency plans in the event of a complete breakdown of law and order and the need to save lives in Cairo and protect the Embassy. In short, they involved the 16th Parachute Brigade landing on the Gezira Club race course and a follow up force of tanks and Bren gun carriers racing up the desert road from the Canal Zone. I was also aware that it was four o'clock, two hours before darkness, which would mean that either operation would have to be aborted soon. A decision would have to be made within minutes. As I stood there the Ambassador wasted no time: 'Is your wireless set up to speak direct to GHQ?' 'Yes,' I said, 'the aerial is up the tree in the garden. The code word to start the operation is "Haybox",' and that was all I needed to say. There was an urgent discussion among those present. I kept my mouth shut. Just at that moment a message was thrust into the Ambassador's hand. The rabble had reached the Semiramis as we knew, but the message read that a policeman had opened fire as the leaders climbed the entrance steps. This was the first armed intervention that day and the effect was immediate. The leaders broke away as their comrades fell. The police moved in to make arrests. The Ambassador held his hand as quietness descended. I never sent my message. Sir Stephen's coolness 'under fire' was in the best tradition of the Diplomatic Service. The whole future of the Middle East would have changed for good had that one word been spoken.

The American Ambassador, whose Embassy lay not far away from where we were all assembled, stood down his detachment of Marines when he heard the news. Needless to say, the British Embassy had no military protection except for the Military, Naval and Air Attachés! There then followed a surprising sequence of events, given the mayhem of the last hours of the day. King Farouk through it all had been entertaining 600 guests at Abdin Palace to celebrate the birth of his son and, as he assumed, his heir. The palace was less than a kilometre from Opera Square. Either the guests did not know what was happening, or, more likely, the King had made it clear what was the most important event of the day and no one dared leave. As night fell, the King, awaking finally to what had happened to his city, gave orders for the army to enter and take control. An immediate curfew was imposed. Any one on the streets would be shot according to the curfew broadcasts which were made every few minutes. The Egyptian army was disciplined and had trained alongside the British army for decades. By six o'clock, within the hour, the city was still burning but silent. The only noise was the rattle of Bren gun carriers, their army's main patrol vehicles like those of the British army, and, as *The Times* so graphically described it, 'the clicking of the heels as soldiers mounted guard at key buildings and street corners'.

Nahas Pasha, after a hurriedly called meeting of the Cabinet, assumed draconian powers as the Military Governor of Egypt, little knowing how short his tenure of office as Prime Minister would be. I drove home rapidly to Zamalek, over the Kasr Nil Bridge using

A western style bar that was targeted in the riots of 26 January 1952. (London Illustrated News, *9 February 1952*)

my Embassy pass, from where I could see the city, still smouldering. Before I left I had been given and announced the death toll. There was an unknown number among the indigenous mixture of races which made up the populations of Cairo and Alexandria, a city which had also suffered. It was estimated that between ten and fifteen thousand of the inhabitants in Cairo alone would lose their employment. Nahas Pasha, in an extraordinary *volte face*, tried to mitigate the ineffective response by his Government to the rioting by saying that he was even more grieved by these riots than the action by the British against the 'auxiliary' police at Ismailia. It was to become a day of intense diplomatic activity led by the American and French Ambassadors calling on Sir Ralph Stevenson who confirmed that he had already sent a note to Farag Pasha, the acting Foreign Minister. In it he reiterated that assurances had been sought to protect foreign nationals to no avail. The British army moved units down the desert road close to the Heliopolis check point to receive and protect foreign nationals fleeing from Cairo by this route. Units in all the towns bordering the Canal Zone were put on alert.

Farouk, to save face, promptly dismissed Nahas Pasha and his whole Cabinet, appointing Ali Maher Pasha, a long term and faithful public servant to the royal family of Egypt, first as Chief of the Royal Cabinet to the late King Fuad, Farouk's father, and later as a Prime Minister in a former administration. While insisting that terrorism should be brought to an end and the lives of British and other nationalities should be protected, the Treaty remained a bone of contention. Ali Maher Pasha made it clear that he would not accept its provisions. With Serag el Din out of office and in hiding and Nahas Pasha disgraced, a whole new political front was created. I was happy to leave my diplomatic friends to deal with the press, to see more of my family and wonder how long it would be before we had another crisis.

In the lull which followed, Sir Ralph Stevenson took the opportunity to write a lengthy report to the Foreign Office on the work of the Information Department since the unilateral abrogation of the 1936 Treaty and all that had followed.[6] He recorded a total of 130 daily, sometimes twice daily, press conferences held by me as the Military Spokesman and his appointed Embassy people. The first press conference had been held on 8 October 1951, when Sir

Roderick 'Roddy' Parkes, head of the Information Department, and I fielded questions from thirty-six correspondents who turned up. At the time they knew more about what was happening than us. I remember the look on their faces when Roddy asked them what they knew! Since then the Ambassador reported that 113 journalists, covering newspapers and other media in sixteen countries had come through my office. An early decision had been taken to deny every outrageous canard published daily by the two leading Wafd papers, *Al Ahram* and *El Misr*. Most of this propaganda came from Serag el Din, backed by Nahas Pasha. In his despatch, Sir John described it as 'out-Goebbeling Goebbels', the Nazi propagandist of the late war whose name had become a derisive household word in British homes when his statements were broadcast on the BBC.

The use of my telephone link to the Canal Zone was officially approved and indeed encouraged. The easing of censorship under the new Government would mean that denials, when needed, could more easily be transmitted through press channels, all of which would relieve me, as I thought, in the future. The main agencies I had always relied on to carry my comments had been Reuters, Agence France Presse, and the Associated Press of America who headed up a strong team of US and local reporters and gave Reuters a run for their money. In their world, a beat of even a few minutes on a story was a feather in the cap, or, if late, a caustic cable from New York. Socratese Chakalas, known to everyone as Soc, became a good friend and I felt that I had been able to put over the British army position to what I knew was, on the whole, an unsympathetic and sometimes hostile American public. On the other hand, Soc never let a friendship get in the way of a 'scoop'.

The one taboo subject for the Egyptian press was any reporting about the King, except in the most favourable terms, such as his intervention finally on 'Black Saturday' to bring in the Egyptian army. This applied equally to foreign journalists. Any probe into his private life would be censored and the journalist might well find himself on the next plane out of Egypt. It was an ironic situation as his self-indulgent behaviour had filled the society columns of the press outside Egypt for many years, and his two marriages had been widely reported on. What had been carefully concealed from all but the close royal circle and those affected was his predilection for seducing young girls. Wives of army officers were at particular risk because the first step after his eyes alighted on his next potential conquest would be a posting for the husband to a remote far flung garrison. The resentment among young officers whose wives were the obvious targets was to lead to his downfall.

Jehan Sadat, whose husband Anwar was to be one of the leaders of the underground movement, describes the fear of the King's attention vividly in her memoirs.[7] Recently married and only eighteen, she had spent a lovely day with her husband in Alexandria. On their way home they were passing the exclusive RAC Club when Anwar said he had to see a Dr Yussef Rashid, the King's personal doctor and head of the Royal Intelligence Service. Also, unknown to many, he was a friend of Anwar's, and he used him from time to time to feed disinformation to the King about the 'Officers' Movement', of which the royal circle had heard rumours. Yussef, in a friendly way, asked him to stay and have dinner with him. Anwar demurred, but Jehan says she saw on the menu her favourite dish, grilled shrimp, the speciality of the Club.

King Farouk with a girlfriend in an Italian nightclub in 1963. Farouk's exile did not alter his appetite for excess.

Anwar, newly married and very much in love, consented to stay and delay getting back to Cairo to please her. She writes in her book, 'I never got to taste them. Shortly after we sat down another party arrived at the next table. I felt the strength of someone's eyes on me. Looking up, I gazed directly into the King's face. I was panic stricken. Whenever he saw a woman he wanted he sent for her – and had her. Here I was face to face with this immoral King. I knew I was not bad looking. I was eighteen, Farouk's favourite age.'[8] The tension mounted. The King sent for Dr Rashid and demanded to know 'who was the girl'. His first answer, 'just friends of mine', did not satisfy. No sooner had he returned to his table than he was sent for again to answer the same question and he gave the same reply. After an interval, he recalled Dr Rashid once again. Anwar was agitated. 'Hurry up and eat', he said, but Jehan writes she was so upset and frightened she could not force down a mouthful. They left as quickly as they could, without raising suspicion. This was just as well. Anwar had only been released two years previously from a period of eight years in and out of prison for subversive activities. It was a long and worrying drive back to Cairo.

The event had hardened Anwar's attitude and, in a meeting with his fellow conspirators, including Abdul Nasser whom he would one day follow as President, the date for the planned Free Officers' Movement was brought forward from 1956 to November 1952. Anwar Sadat, writing in his book *Revolt on the Nile*, says that rumours that Farouk had been greatly alarmed by the events of Black Saturday, and might even leave Egypt under certain conditions, caused the junta to bring forward the date again, to July 1952. This was the date that eventually brought about the abdication of Farouk.

For those of us still reeling from the effect of the riots, we could only sit by and monitor the press coverage which was revealed as the papers, showing the dramatic pictures of a burning city, reached us from England and overseas countries. The Embassy faced a delicate situation with a new Prime Minister challenging the terms of the Treaty, and at the same time being required to emphasise the importance of maintaining a strong military presence in the Middle East. It was a difficult balance to achieve in the face of now often hostile questions from the international press still based in Cairo. I was to be greatly helped by a new diplomat who joined our team and answered some of these questions.

Arthur Kellas was a former soldier in the Parachute Regiment and an 'arabist'. He had a distinguished war record and went down well with the press. He was able to make diplomatic comments against a military background, which I encouraged. So it was a sad day for me when some six months after the upheaval of the coup d'état and with Cairo hitting the headlines again, he fell into the trap of answering a press question without prefacing one of his remarks as 'off the record'. He had been asked for the Embassy's reaction to a hysterical outburst by Nasser condemning the British 'occupation', while secretly negotiating for a substantial loan from the British Government. This was too much for Arthur who could not resist quoting an old Arab proverb, 'the dog barks but the caravan moves on'. Declared 'persona non grata', within a few days he had left Egypt. He had had to go so quickly that, when meeting him by chance in London some time later, he was still driving his car carrying Egyptian number plates.

The fall of Nahas Pasha and the appointment of a new Prime Minister who continued to keep the Egyptian army in control of Cairo and the principal cities gave a breathing space for the British army, up to a point. The interest of the press also continued to focus on the political front. A consultative Council had been formed to take the opposition to the Anglo-Egyptian Treaty further. It contained two members of the old Wafd Party, Serag el Din Pasha, who had held the title of Foreign Minister in the former government but had spent his time at the United Nations Assembly in Paris, and his 'stand in' during that time, Ibrahim Farag, who had remained in Cairo. Their inclusion was meant to indicate an 'all party' approach with other members from the more liberal and Saadist parties; a very modern approach to constitutional reform which would have been anathema to the old regime and Farouk tucked up in his palace. Inevitably it was to fail as public opinion turned against the Wafd members. The new regime's Director of Prosecutions arrested many of the perpetrators of the riots and leading politicians such as Serag el Din. In none of the reporting following the riots and burning and analysis of the events leading up to it was there any mention of the Free Officers' Movement or of Sadat or Nasser. From the tone of Sadat's quick call to his wife at the start, it seems clear that the riots had caught the Movement by surprise and they had not wanted any publicity at that stage.[9] It was remarkable that the press had not penetrated it, or, if they had, that they kept it under wraps. I knew nothing of this 'movement' at the time, and yet I could not believe that 'Sammy' Sansom with his intelligence links was not up to speed on this.

From the army viewpoint one good result was the calling off of the long strike by dock workers at Port Said, enabling army stores to be moved once again. The Governor of Port Said confirmed that he would not tolerate intimidation of workers now returning, and denied that his powers under martial law had been used to break the strike.[10] For the Royal Navy it meant that the much needed cruiser HMS *Cleopatra* could be relieved of providing mooring crews and general harbour duties.

The situation in the Canal Zone came briefly into the news again when *The Times* achieved something of a coup by its reporter stationed there, who became involved in a rescue operation to retrieve the bodies of two pilots from a crashed Royal Air Force Mosquito fighter bomber.[11] It had come down in the swampy area south-west of Port Said. The first rescue attempt had been made by soldiers from the 1st Battalion of the Oxford and Buckinghamshire Light Infantry, 'Ox and Bucks' to the rest of the army. They had to give up a mile from the crash site after struggling all night through a salt water marsh using makeshift pontoons. A final attempt, with *The Times* 'at the front', found a dead pilot but no sign of his companion. So the casualties from the unilateral abrogation of the Treaty mounted; an event which would have just been passed by if it had not been for *The Times*. For all the calumny aimed at the press by senior officers for 'getting in the way' and sometimes being critical of military action, were it not for the journalists, often risking their own lives to get the news, so much of what the forces do for their country would pass unnoticed.

In Cairo a sort of peace reigned. The press corps began to disperse and the social life which I had looked forward to on being posted from Kenya began to return. The Semiramis Hotel, recovering from its fright of nearly being burnt, resumed its dinner dances on the roof-top terrace, and repair work had already started on many of the fire struck buildings. It was a time for reflection too, on how we had handled the influx of the media at short notice and with an inadequate staff. We came to the conclusion that, if the armed forces needed a 'reserve', so did the information departments. Updating the figures since the Ambassador's last report to the Foreign Office, we calculated that by

3 February 1952, 177 journalists representing 110 media outlets in twenty countries had attended our press conferences and been briefed at one time or another. One military lesson which had been learnt was the need for a mobile reserve on stand-by, to meet international obligations or a crisis effecting British interests and citizens. The possibility of the army having to occupy Cairo again had been very real. Despite the considerable forces available then in the Canal Zone, such a move would have depleted forces sufficient to protect and operate the base and, by definition, Middle East security. A mobile reserve was therefore brought into being. It would be spearheaded by the 1st Battalion the Coldstream Guards, already on their way to Port Said as an advance guard of 32 Guards Brigade. This force would eventually comprise the Coldstreams, the 1st Battalion the Scots Guards, and the 1st Battalion the Bedfordshire and Hertfordshire Regiments; a total of three Infantry Battalions, some 3,000 men with an armoured element. These are figures which could not be imagined by army commanders today. The Defence Budget of 1952 was in support of some 500,000 men. No such figure would ever be contemplated again, not even after Suez and the humiliation of that debacle four years later, or even the successful recapture of the Falklands.

The death of King George VI on 5 February 1952, following a long period of ill health, still came as a shock to the expatriates living in Egypt, many who may not have been home for years. For the diplomatic service, the death of a Monarch institutes a series of recognised procedures abroad, as well as in the home country, including all countries with diplomatic recognition. The formalities often give diplomats the opportunity for informal meetings, but in Cairo, and even with King Farouk, one would not have expected an invitation for the wives of the British Embassy staff, from the highest to the lowest, to Abdin Palace to 'sign the book', congratulating his Queen on the birth of her son. Such an invitation, despite being in mourning for the death of their King, could not be avoided. So it was that Embassy wives, mine included, duly arrived at the Palace clad in black. But the diplomatic niceties were observed on both sides, with the wives of the Court draped in Dior evening clothes of mauve and pink, their colours of mourning out of respect for the late King. As my wife said to me later, we felt like twenty-four blackbirds in a pie while we drank rose hip syrup.

CHAPTER EIGHT

King Farouk Abdicates

While I was at GHQ in the Canal Zone reviewing the press situation with Jock Carroll, I met up with an old friend from the regiment, Major 'Reggie' Guy, holed up in a miserable part of the Zone. It was *de rigueur* that anyone visiting from Cairo brought fresh fruit and vegetables which were always gratefully received as a change from the usual army Catering Corps rations. Suddenly, while there I was sent for once again and told to go back to Cairo at once.

It was the first week of March 1952. Ali Maher, reigning Prime Minister, deserted by two senior ministers and blocked from calling a recess of Parliament to sort things out, had resigned. We were back to riding the political roundabout once again. It had all been about obtaining a vote of Parliament to go into recess for a month. Another Egyptian figure from the past, Hilaly Pasha, another lawyer, emerged as Prime Minister. The turn around was so quick that the Ambassador, due to call on the resigning PM that same morning, cancelled the appointment using the well worn diplomatic 'flu' excuse.

On 23 July the roundabout ground to a halt. It would be many years before politicians once again commanded any attention. An Egyptian royal family would be a thing of the past. King Farouk might continue to attract the society columnists of those in the press who looked to a night-clubbing, self-indulgent Monarch to increase their circulation, but he would never set foot in Egypt again.

It started at 6.15 in the morning while I was dozing before facing, as I thought, another quiet day in the office. All but the regular Cairo based correspondents had left, bored with the political stories. Patrick Smith of the BBC, with his office close to mine, was one of the 'stickers'. It was his well known voice that woke me up as I grabbed the phone. 'You had better get down here quickly,' he said, 'there are tanks and troops everywhere on the streets and the Cable and Wireless offices are shut down'. Throwing on some clothes and hoping my car outside would be in one piece, I drove once again over Kasr Nil Bridge, passing what was left of the old colonial barracks at full speed, turning sharp right and slamming on the brakes outside the office. There was no sign of soldiers; whatever was happening, it was not a riot requiring protection of the diplomatic quarter. I opened Patrick's door. He waved me to be silent. He was listening to a local broadcast. It finished and Patrick said 'it's a coup d'état. That was some army Colonel called Sadat who said he was speaking on behalf of a General Neguib. He is telling everyone to keep calm.' Some hope, I thought, after the riots of January. But then Patrick held up his hand again as the radio came on. 'The Egyptian army has taken over', the voice continued. I revised my opinion but clearly the press would be hammering on my door very quickly if Cable and Wireless was closed down and the only other means of getting the news out was through a censored telephone exchange or my subversive line via Ismailia. It was a few minutes past 7 a.m. My clerk had heard the broadcast. I set up the operation to get through to Jock Carroll in the Canal Zone. 'What the devil are you doing ringing me up before breakfast?' was his curt reply. I gave a brief run-down of what Patrick had told me, and that communications in Cairo had been cut. We had to open the Ismailia line again for the press to report the coup d'état. 'It is a real emergency and all the Cairo press will be banging on my door for help,' I said. 'I didn't know Royal Signals had stopped transmitting press copy via the War Office,' he replied, 'leave it to me.' Half an hour later the phone rang and Jock's number two was on the line, which proved the line was open both ways. He said, 'It's all fixed and I have sent Patrick's despatch to the BBC by Royal Signals.' My heart stopped. I said 'That was not Patrick's proper despatch but only what he thought was happening and told me.' 'Well it's gone and I cannot get it back' and as usual the line went dead. When I told Patrick, he just went quiet and said 'well, if it isn't a coup by the army that's the end for me. For goodness sake ring back and send another saying "KILL KILL KILL ALL" filing full story.' I told him sorry I could not as my line had gone dead. The news agencies were frantic with even Haigh Nicholson at Reuters, and Soc at Associated Press of America, who had never risked using my line, begging for help. Then a messenger from the Embassy rushed in carrying their translation of Sadat's broadcast, a script which I let everyone read. Photo copying had not then been invented. We only had 'roneo', too slow for the press. It read:

> To my brothers the sons of the Nile:
>
> You know that our country has been living through delicate moments and you have seen the hands of traitors at work in its affairs. These traitors dared to extend their influence to the Army, imagining that it was devoid of patriotic elements.
>
> We have therefore decided to purify ourselves, to eliminate the traitors and weaklings, and thus record a new and honourable page in the history of our country. Those who engage in destructive activities will be severely punished. The Army will co-operate with the Police in maintaining order.
>
> In conclusion, I would like to reassure our brothers, the foreigners who live among us, that their interests will be respected. We will be fully responsible for their lives and property.

There was no doubt that the Egyptian army was in control. No rioting was reported to me from correspondents watching the streets. This was a complete contrast to seven months before. Into the relative calm now of my office, with Cable and Wireless working once again, a smiling Patrick Smith came waving a cable form. It was from the foreign editor of BBC World Service. 'Go on, read it to me,' I said. It was short and to the point: 'Congratulations your world scoop'. Still grinning he said, 'back to the office – I'm doing a background piece for tonight.'

There was little doubt that he had influenced the world press with my early morning message of a coup d'état in Egypt. Sometime later I

Nasser (seated second to right) and Neguib (seated right) at a press conference shortly after the coup d'état.

got hold of *The Times* sent to the Embassy, and the headline for that day read:

GENERAL NEGUIB MOHAMMED'S COUP D'ETAT.
ANTI-CORRUPTION AIMS IN EGYPT.

The report quoted him as saying that his object was to end the instability of government and corruption in high places. He had no foreign aims.

Major-General Neguib, his rank at the time, had been selected by the military junta led by Sadat and Nasser, both junior army officers, to lead the coup by virtue of his authority in the army. He had come to prominence when he put himself forward, at Nasser's suggestion, for the presidency of the Military Club. This was dominated by Farouk who always nominated a senior sycophantic officer and was never challenged in his choice. Not this time; with overwhelming votes, Neguib was appointed so that at the time of the coup he held a position of prestige in the army, able to overrule those senior to him at the time. By the age of fifty he had achieved the rank of

Major-General. He had visited England and France in 1939, where he inspected the Maginot Line which was thought would hold back the German army! Although the army had not been involved directly in the desert war just past, Neguib had 'filled in' as an acting Brigade Major when on attachment and the regular British officer became ill. He had fought with distinction in the Palestine war and was wounded. But the junta had miscalculated the extent of his ambition. Having secured the position as leader of the coup, despite being considered a mere puppet, it was to be a very long time before Nasser and Sadat would come into their own as the true leaders of the revolutionary movement.

Detail from picture on p. 67. (*Mirrorpix*)

CHAPTER NINE

King Farouk Trapped in Alexandria

In Cairo, details began to emerge of the traumatic events in Alexandria since the broadcast by Sadat early on the morning of 23 July. We learnt that General Neguib had arrived there from Cairo. The King was in his summer palace beside the sea. There were no reports of any shooting that morning but the palace had been surrounded by soldiers, as had the Cairo Palace. That the coup eventually would lead to the demise of the Muhammed Ali ruling family, with its historical rights, and to the loss of the crown for Farouk's own son, was such a remote possibility in Farouk's mind that he set about restoring his authority as though this was a distraction in his otherwise pleasurable life. It was a matter of pacifying the Officers' Movement of which he was aware, but had never given much credence.[1]

First he acceded to the appointment of Ali Maher as Prime Minister, whom he had dismissed after the riots of 26 January, knowing him to be favourable towards the Officers' Movement. Then he confirmed the appointment of Major-General Neguib to be Commander-in-Chief of the armed forces with the rank of Lieutenant-General, despite having had his own nomination over-ridden at the Officers' Military Club meeting. It was to no avail. Further humiliation was heaped upon him as the junta demands were made. In rapid succession he accepted the resignation of the Brigadier commanding the Royal Body Guard, the Air Force Commodore who was his ADC, the Master of the Works for the Royal Palaces (knowing all that was in them) and finally his own physician. Arrests started taking place by order of the new Prime Minister. These included the Commandant of the Cairo Police, the Director of the Political Bureau of the Ministry of the Interior and his Secretary of State, a Major-General. This presaged a major purge of the army with officers being placed under close arrest, including, significantly, the Commandant of the Frontier Forces, under whom Sadat had served. All this took place within two days of the surrounding of the palaces in Alexandria and Cairo.

Lieutenant-General Neguib, as Commander-in-Chief, also made his presence felt by driving through Alexandria in an open car visiting troops. Driving to the Mustapha Barracks and acknowledging the good wishes of the assembled crowds on his way, he then met formally the new Prime Minister, Ali Maher. It must be said that shortly after the departure of the King he relinquished, as a matter of principle, his new rank, reverting to Major-General and, with it, the loss of salary, the former rank carrying the remuneration of a Cabinet Minister. It was at this meeting with the new Prime Minister that the Abdication Document was drafted and agreed it should be released with its full text at six o' clock on the evening of 26 July. It would come as a terrible shock to Farouk and his entourage, and indeed to Royalist support amongst the ruling classes. That the King had acceded to the stringent demands so readily was probably due to the inclusion of the clause allowing his son to become King under a Regency. It was calculated by the junta that this would placate any Royalist movement and reassure the international community of the stability of the new Government. This was a clever move, robbing Farouk of any chance of a come-back. The exact wording to which Farouk had put his name was: 'in compliance with the wishes of the people we have decided to abdicate in favour of our son Crown Prince Ahmed Fuad II'.

The smooth operation at day two of the coup was vindication of the pragmatic planning by the junta, placing the well respected General Neguib at the forefront of the revolutionary movement and preventing bloodshed. But friction between Anwar Sadat and Neguib, both in Alexandria at the same time, rapidly escalated as Neguib was hailed internationally as the leader of the revolution.[2]

Popular support for General Neguib, October 1952.

Nasser, reading the headlines in Cairo, was equally disturbed. It had been envisaged by the Command Revolutionary Council that Nasser was to be hailed as the leader behind the coup, while Neguib was to be the public face – a homely, pleasant, smiling face that would appeal to foreign diplomats, reporters and cameramen. I was to meet Anwar much later, under strange circumstances, then to become friends, exchanging meetings between wives as well and his English mother-in-law. To the press in Cairo and Alexandria, however, he was virtually unknown, although Sammy Sansom at the Embassy must have known about the subversive Free Officers' Movement during the 1939–45 war when Sadat had been involved and imprisoned for spying.[3] I could only suppose I had been kept in the dark because I was tarred with the same brush as the press; not to be trusted with confidential information.

In Alexandria, events were moving quickly to a climax. Michael Cresswell, the Minister at the Embassy, was acting for Sir Ralph who was on leave in the UK. Accompanied by Brigadier Goulburn in full dress uniform, they had called on Ali Maher, the new Prime Minister, on the morning of 28 July. The meeting lasted an hour. The message being given by them was the same as Arthur Kellas in our information offices was giving to the Egyptian Press and foreign correspondents. The United Kingdom had not interfered in the internal affairs of Egypt and would not do so unless lives and property of British residents were put at risk. All I could add was that while the British army was always on the alert, no threatening moves had been made and the troops were still within the Canal Zone.

Cresswell and Brigadier Goulburn then met with Anwar Sadat at the Mustapha Pasha Barracks where he was with some of the military members of what one would call today the 'Revolutionary Council', but had been named the 'Constitutional Council', another of Nasser's euphemisms. It was a tense meeting. Sadat, confronted by the Brigadier in his imposing uniform, wrote later, 'It was in the old Imperial manner which the British used to frighten their Colonial leaders'.[4] He followed this by demanding that the assurances given by Michael Cresswell on the role of British forces be put in writing as a formal note from the British Government. He also refutes, in the same book, the statement allegedly made that 'Muhammed Ali was the ruling family of Egypt with its rights and that Farouk's son would follow in succession to Farouk.' He writes that he challenged Michael Cresswell and the Brigadier as though they had made it. 'Surely it is nothing to do with you? It is not a British ruling family is it?' He reported to the 'Cairo Command' that the first confrontation with Britain had taken place at midday on 26 July and it would end in Britain's complete retreat.

The meeting with Sadat was not reported by Arthur Kellas to the press acting as the Embassy spokesman. We still only knew of Sadat from the early morning broadcast announcing the coup d'état. Nor did we know in Cairo of the pressure being put upon Sadat to expel the King from the shores of Egypt. Nasser had given orders that the King was to be expelled today, that was the day before the meeting at the Mustapha Pasha Barracks. Sadat had done his best but the troops at his disposal were tired and the officer commanding would not commit them to a midnight operation. Sadat had no authority to over-rule him. They did take up positions round both palaces at 8 a.m. the following morning, knowing the King was in one of them. Sadat had been all set to go with his battle cry: 'We have been waiting for this for ten years. We adopted the slogan Resolution and Boldness. The password is Nasser. Zero Hour – Midnight.'[5] Nasser too was under

Abdul Nasser.

pressure to remove Farouk from Egypt as soon as possible after an all
night session of the Council. There had been hours of debate on what
to do with Farouk, and death had been on the agenda, but Nasser,
when a younger man, had been under the influence of the Moslem
Brotherhood and had watched an assassination. He had had to
listen to the screams of the victim's wife. He vowed never to witness
another.[6] He also knew the international implications of such a move
better than anyone. Farouk would never know his life had been saved
by Nasser, nor would he know the reason for his immediate forced
departure when he had let it be known that he might abdicate in his
own time.

Sadat moved fast on the morning of the 26th with General Neguib,
driving through the night from Cairo, once Nasser had put everything
in train. After he had assumed power, President Neguib was to claim, in
disagreement with Sadat, that he had been at the centre of the planning
throughout. In fact the junta had a tiger by the tail. It was to be many
years before Nasser would able to claim his rightful reward to become
President after removing Neguib. The abdication papers were signed
by Farouk and Neguib at 10 a.m. on 26 July 1952 (Appendix One).
Anwar Sadat told Jehan that Farouk had signed them twice with a
trembling hand, having misspelled his name in Arabic the first time.
Jehan commentated later in her book recording all this: 'it was proof
positive that he was a foreigner through and through.'[7]

The King had been given until six o'clock that same evening to
leave his palace and board the royal yacht *Marhroussa*, standing
by at the docks. Whatever his other failings, he was good packer.
In the short time available one observer saw 204 pieces of luggage
leave the dockside. There was little doubt in the minds of the junta
that he had already stashed away a fortune in foreign banks but they
had ensured that everything he left behind in Egypt was lost to him.
Jehan, with a woman's attention to detail, records that the final figure
at Sotheby's auction house for his confiscated property was £E70
million. It was used to establish health centres and schools, much
under the supervision of Jehan herself.[8]

Precisely on the hour, Farouk, no longer the King, left the jetty and
boarded the royal yacht, accompanied by his wife, two daughters and
his infant son, King Fuad II, never to reign in Egypt. General Neguib
had dithered between going aboard the yacht to say farewell or board

a battleship of the Egyptian Royal Navy standing by to watch the ex-royal family depart. At the last moment he chose the yacht, but, his driver losing his way, he was left clambering up a 'Jacob's Ladder' to say his last few words. There was a last minute scare as rumours circulated among the small crowd watching that the Coast Guard would open fire on the yacht, but Anwar Sadat had ordered a formal parade to be mounted by a contingent of the Egyptian Royal Air Force as a mark of respect to prevent any last minute demonstrations.

Neguib left no time before establishing himself as the prime mover in all this. As the yacht sailed away he was already at the microphone of the local broadcasting studio in Alexandria speaking to the 'people':

> To the Egyptian people, my fellow countrymen: To complete the work which your valiant army has undertaken for your cause I met today Ali Maher Pasha your Prime Minister and handed him a petition directed to His Majesty Farouk I containing two demands from the people. First: to abdicate in favour of His Highness the Crown Prince by noon today; and second: to leave the country by six o'clock today. His Majesty graciously agreed to the two demands which were carried out without any untoward incident.

In Cairo the broadcast not only put Neguib forward as the leader of the revolution, but stirred up, as Jehan writes, 'a spontaneous outburst of singing and dancing in the streets'.[9] Unaware of all that had gone on in Alexandria, and not having heard from Anwar before the broadcast, she was on her way to a late evening appointment with her dentist in down town Cairo. Upon arrival she was immediately put in front of everyone else waiting. Protesting at this favourable treatment, the dentist (himself in the army) said 'have you not heard Mrs Sadat? The army has expelled the King. Your husband is now one of the leaders of Egypt'. Leaving at once, she dashed into the streets to join in the celebrations. That she would one day be the wife of a President of Egypt could never, at eighteen, have entered her head that day. Nor that she would play a leading role among the world leaders, supporting the emancipation of women in Egypt and influencing leaders in other Arab countries.[10] The broadcast and Neguib's fondness for driving afterwards in an open car to receive the cheers of the people were to lead to a deep seated rift between the instigators of the revolution and Neguib.

Newspaper cutting from *The Times*,
31 December 1952, showing the author
(right) talking to General Neguib (left).

CHAPTER TEN

The Aftermath:
Meetings with Sadat and Neguib

It would not be until four years later, when Neguib published his book,[1] that the inside story of the lead up to the coup d'état became public, with Anwar Sadat refuting Neguib's version by the publication of his own book two years later.[2] In it he sharply refutes Neguib's claim to have master minded the Abdication operation from the start. 'I was at all times in actual command but my movements were being closely watched. I would have jeopardised our chances of success had I attempted to play an active role. It was agreed that I should remain at home until the first phase of the revolt had been completed. Only then would I join my colleagues'. Sadat makes it clear that while he was in Alexandria, Neguib was in bed and did not arrive at Nasser's HQ in the Kubra el Kubba Barracks until all had been settled and the order given for Sadat to make the important broadcast. He asserts that the broadcast had to be in Neguib's name to follow Nasser's strategy of using him as the front man. There was no doubt in the minds of either authors, though they were both unwilling to admit that it was in fact Nasser who had master-minded the whole operation. He was to bide his time and eventually remove Neguib.

In the first few months of his presidency, Neguib did not endear himself to the supporters of Anwar Sadat; they felt Sadat had a right to more recognition for his role in Alexandria, a feeling that Jehan

Abdul Nasser (left) with General
Neguib (right), October 1952.

shared. So when Neguib, driving through Cairo in his open car, his
favourite method of travel, waving to the pedestrians as he passed,
suddenly decided to pull up outside Jehan's parent's house, her
reaction was immediate. 'Run down and tell the President there is no
one at home', she said to their maid. 'Tell him you do not expect me
back for many hours'.[3] This was a wise judgement for a girl of just
eighteen or nineteen – evidence of the ability and courage she was to
show on the death of her husband Anwar, and during the subsequent
years when she played such an important role within Egypt and on
the international stage.

For my part, I expected a quiet time in the weeks following the
coup after all the international press coverage and the press corps
had drifted away. I was taken aback, therefore, at the continued
hostility of the two main papers, *El Misr* and *Al Ahram*, and a new
publication *El Gumhuriyya*, which my erudite colleague translated
as 'The Republic'. I found myself back to the old routine of denying
or correcting reports on the alleged activities of the army in the Canal
Zone reported in these publications.

Then, on one of these routine days, my clerk came into the office while I was on the phone as usual, urgently signalling to me that he must speak. I put the phone down and said 'Well what's the problem?' 'Colonel Anwar Sadat wants to meet you', he said in a breathless voice. I thought back to that early morning broadcast which Patrick Smith and I had heard. We had later sought to find out more about this person whose importance was surely to be judged by his announcement of the coup d'état. Not much had been forthcoming from the Embassy, which, typically impressed by rank, was taken up with their diplomatic overtures to General Neguib. The assumption was that Anwar Sadat, a mere 'half' Colonel like myself, was in some way a subordinate officer in the Egyptian army, and worse, connected with the press; not worthy of the attention of a Brigadier Military Attaché. I was very used to this sort of denigration. It gave me a free hand to respond to the message without consultation. 'Yes' I said, 'where and when?' The answer came back that I should meet him after midnight at the Badia night club. He would be in uniform. My first reaction was to check that this famous night club had been repaired sufficiently after the arson attacks of 26 January 1951. Was there some hidden message behind this location? I had little time to find out and just hoped that my wife would believe this was not an excuse for me to watch the belly dancing for which the Badia had been renowned 'in the good old days' (one particular dancer known as Fatima was as famous as any film star of that time in the Middle East).

So, in plain clothes – I had not worn uniform since the abrogation of the 1936 Treaty – I entered a smoke filled room encircling a dance floor where belly dancing was most certainly taking place, but not, perhaps, by the famous Fatima. I stayed still until my eyes became used to the semi-darkness, but no one approached me. I felt at least there would have been message, but on reflection I realised that in no way would Sadat have said 'I am meeting a Colonel Hornby show him to my table'. So I just stood there and looked round the tables at the back of the room. I was looking for someone in uniform. I found such a man smoking heavily, almost concealed by tobacco smoke, and walked up to the table, presuming it was Colonel Sadat. He gestured to the only other chair. I held out my hand and we both took firm grips. There was no friction. We were both of the same rank and

Anwar Sadat, editor of *El Gumhuriyya*, at the time of his friendship with the author.

within a few months of the same age and service. We immediately did what most army people do which is to talk about service contacts, where we have served and our families. I mentioned the war knowing nothing of course then about his spying activities on behalf of Rommel and the German Command, nor that he been imprisoned for eight years as a result. I was glad not to know then, and I only found out upon the publication of his book about his early life.

Now I was sitting in a smoke filled basement talking to an Egyptian officer after a coup d'état. I learnt that he was married and had a young bride. I said that I had had very little time with my family over the past eighteen months and was kept at the telephone night and day, seven days a week, checking stories mainly in the two newspapers *El Misr* and *Al Ahram* about the activities of the army in the Canal Zone. I said it was an old British army custom to try and get home for weekends. My children hardly ever saw me, I said, laying it on thick. I think I struck a chord as he agreed that family was very important. I must say that later, having met his most attractive wife, I was not surprised that he too would like to spend more time at home. I put it to him that if he made no statements on a Friday, his day of religious observance, I would follow suit and say nothing of substance to the press until after mine, on a Sunday. He agreed and we went on to discuss the desert war, still fresh in our minds, and the fact that Rommel had so nearly got to Cairo. He remarked bitterly that the British army never let the Egyptian army go into combat. 'We were confined to communications', he said, and then revealed that he had been in Signals after a specialist course of which he was obviously proud. I thought we parted friends in the early hours of the morning. I had never been briefed by the Embassy and saw no reason to report in detail of my meeting. I accepted Anwar Sadat as a fellow officer, and our subsequent family meetings, when we came to know his wife Jehan and her English mother, all confirmed my first impression that he was a fine officer destined for a senior rank in his army, and with whom I would have been willing to serve had he been in the British army. That he would one day be President of Egypt, only to be assassinated by the Moslem Brotherhood, was beyond comprehension then. As was his history as a spy for the Germans in their advance on Cairo, his resultant two terms of imprisonment over eight years, and his formation of the Free Officers' Movement with Nasser as early as 1939, with its patriotic ambition of removing Farouk and the British from Egypt. I had to wait twenty-eight years to read this in his book *In search of Identity.*[4]

To say that as a result of my midnight meeting all was to be sweetness and light between my office and the Egyptian press would have been wishful thinking. In fact, I learnt later that he was the editor of the new Arabic paper *El Gumhuriyya* (*The Republic*), publishing highly charged patriotic stories of heroic deeds against the 'occupying forces'. However, the weekend truce of not making statements and counter statements seemed to be working. It was a happy time for me to see more of my wife and two girls. When my wife Jean and the girls, aged nine and five, were invited to a house on Roda Island to meet Sadat's wife and her English mother I accepted at once. The thought of informing the Embassy staff who, in any case, were still taken up with their splendid relationship with Neguib never entered my mind.

As we entered the hall of a well appointed and apparently large house, I looked up and there, coming down a slightly curved stair

Anwar and Jehan Sadat.

case, was one of the prettiest girls I had seen in Cairo. I quickly averted my eyes in respect of Islamic culture, of which I had learnt a little during the short time in Egypt. But there was no embarrassment. She was dressed as one would have expected of a wife in an English setting, receiving guests at home for the weekends. The reason for this visit was to meet her English mother who, incidentally, had also called her daughter Jean, Jehan in Arabic. I left at once seeing Jehan greet the children and my wife, taking them by the hand and climbing the stairs. It was only on the publication of her book, *A Woman of Egypt* (Bloomsbury, 1987), that I learnt the story of how her mother, of whom she writes movingly, came to spend her life in Cairo.⁵ Knowing nothing of all this at the time, and reacting to the invitation as the hospitality of one officer to another serving in a foreign land, I was eager to hear how it had all gone. My Jean said she had the impression that she was the first Englishwoman Jehan's mother had spoken to in many years. She had lived in Sheffield and met her husband when he was a student at Sheffield University. Her fear, of which she spoke about to my wife, was of being divorced merely by a husband repeating three times 'I divorce you' in Arabic, 'talaq-talaq-talaq'. They had talked about marriage and children and domestic life. My wife took no notes and I certainly was not going to treat the occasion as anything other than a gesture of goodwill from both Jehan and Anwar. I hoped that, in accordance to army custom, they would accept an invitation to visit us in Zamalek. My elder daughter, many years later, recalls 'drinking tea and something else out of tiny cups'. The family was all returned safely home by Tantawi, my Sudanese driver, without whom I would never have found the house.

I was glad, then, that I had not been briefed by Sammy Sansom, the Embassy Security Officer, who, I learnt later from his book *I Spied Spies*,⁶ had been the one who had arrested Sadat for spying for Germany at the height of the desert war. Having only been fully released a few years before I met him, Sadat's attitude to me as an officer of the British army seemed all the more remarkable. There was a rumour circulating among the press that his original prison term and conditions of confinement had been modified at the insistence of Churchill. At the time of his arrest he could not have imagined that his imprisonment would qualify him, as with so many other nationalist leaders, for the highest office in his country. Had Sansom briefed his superiors before the recent coup took place? This was doubtful as Sadat was unknown in the current diplomatic circles, as was the part he had played in the downfall of Farouk. Sansom's book, *I Spied Spies* (Harrap & Co., 1965), did reveal that Sadat had become involved in the revolutionary movement as early as 1938.

He was picked out as an officer candidate to meet the expansion of the Egyptian army under the 1936 Anglo-Egyptian Treaty, and as someone from the lowest ranks of Egyptian society at the time he was one the few allowed to attend the prestigious Military Academy, hitherto reserved only for the scions of the country's middle and upper classes. Jehan Sadat describes graphically his humble beginnings: 'His Father's salary barely kept bread in the mouths of the thirteen children of the marriage and Anwar spent his entire daily allowance on one glass of milky tea'.[7] Passing a Royal Palace every day on his way to school, where even to touch the flowers belonging to the King could mean imprisonment and maybe death, the seeds of revolt were sown. Sadat's appointment to the Military College, and his subsequent meeting with a fellow cadet Gamel Abdul Nasser from a middle class and very dissimilar background sealed Farouk's fate. Nasser and Sadat became friends, both adopting revolutionary ideals. It took fourteen years of their association to start the Free Officers' Movement and achieve the coup of 1952.

With the return of the Ambassador, Sir Ralph Stevenson, who had been in London throughout the abdication crisis, Cairo was in the news once again. It started with his first visit to the new Prime Minister. According to *The Times* of 28 July, he also met General Neguib for the first time, a meeting lasting forty-five minutes, followed later in the evening for a further half an hour during a break of a four hour session between Neguib and Ali Maher Pasha, the Prime Minister. As I learnt all of this later from *The Times*, and much else during the whole abdication period in Alexandria, I asked myself whether there was any other paper published in the world that could match *The Times* for its detailed and accurate reporting in the midst of world headlines. I relied on the newspaper greatly in trying to produce a chronological sequence of events. In the same way I also learnt of the activities of the American Ambassador, Jefferson Cafferty, and his staff on the day of the abdication. It was well known that there was traditional American support for any moves which would bring about the demise of British influence in the Middle East, linked, as it was, in their minds to our abhorred colonial past. But what was surprising, given the American attitude to monarchy, was Cafferty's close relationship with King Farouk. It was also reported that Cafferty had met Farouk during the day of the abdication. By incorporating the second name of Thomas Jefferson as his first name, one of my friends told me, he revealed his sympathy with revolutionary movements following in the steps of America's declaration of independence.

My own relationship with the American press had been good from the outset, mainly due to Soc Chakalas, Chief of the Associated Press bureau in Cairo, who seemed to take to me as a typical 'limey'. I always treated him equally for the release of press statements with his main competitor, Haigh Nicholson of Reuters. The United States of America were also well covered by visiting correspondents. Listing these towards the end of my stint I was amazed at the coverage they represented: *Chicago Daily News, Chicago Herald Tribune, Christian Science Monitor, Cleveland Plain Dealer, Columbia Broadcasting and TV-News, The New York Times* – which had six correspondents, including their ace reporter, Sirus Sulzberger, chief foreign correspondent – *The New York Herald Tribune, NBC of America*, the *Washington Evening Star*, and the *Wall Street Journal*.

Writing many years later, Barrie St Clare McBride refers to a verbatim exchange of greetings between Jefferson Cafferty's personal secretary in Alexandria, Robert Simpson, and Farouk at 11 a.m. on the fateful day.[8] He had been standing in the corridor outside the reception room for more than an hour where Farouk was meeting Ali Maher. He was spotted during a break, 'Come in, come in,' called Farouk. 'I have never been so glad to see anyone in my life. We haven't much time. I have just two things to tell your Ambassador. Ask him if he will do what he can to save my life – if he does will he come to say goodbye.' The heavy-weight presence of the American press and their coverage, combined with the reports of *The Times* and other British papers, of this last minute meeting, all placed Cafferty in Alexandria and in touch with Farouk, but the exchange of words which passed between the King and his secretary Robert Simpson were unreported at the time. McBride claims that this was indicative of the close relationship which the Ambassador had developed with Farouk and those he later developed with Sadat and Nasser, both of whom he promptly invited to dinner after the abdication.

All this was aimed at reducing the influence of the British in Egypt and the Middle East. This was to manifest itself when Nasser succeeded Neguib, finally to become President of Egypt and fulfil his original ambition in launching the coup d'état. The move he then made to nationalise the Suez Canal, effectively blocking sea traffic to the Far East, was a belligerent response to Eden's Government, the excuse being the withdrawal of financial help to build the Aswan Dam. Nasser's increasingly close relationship with the Soviet Union also persuaded Eden, together with Israel, to make the abortive attempt to retake control of the Suez Canal base, so precipitately abandoned earlier under Egyptian and American pressure.

The Americans were dismayed by the possibility that a 'free Egypt' might come once again under 'colonial rule'. Serving at the Supreme Headquarters of the Allied Powers Europe (SHAPE) in Paris at that time, I was to watch the American General Grunther struggling to be impartial as Supreme Allied Commander of fourteen nations' forces, including his own and those of Great Britain. At the same time the American Sixth Fleet was sailing independently of his command to track the Allied British Forces invasion fleet. To add to Grunther's discomfort, his 'deputy' was Viscount Montgomery who, on principle, never visited SHAPE in that role, maintaining a separate 'court' in Paris. However, in the early hours of one morning Montgomery did so at the urgent request, in confidence, of the senior British officer when three unidentified aircraft were reported flying over Turkey from the east in the direction of France, possibly from the Soviet Union. General Grunther, who had never commanded in war and was more of an administrator and public relations man, was striding up and down with his fingers hovering over the nuclear button, hence the secret British summons for 'Monty'. I was at the door when he walked into the ops room in the full battledress of the most senior officer of the British army, wearing his famous Australian bush hat as headgear with its regimental badges of the wartime army he had commanded. A silence descended on the room. 'Show me the map and location,' he snapped, in that commanding nasal tone which made junior officers jump. With a look and a pause, his sole observation with no further questions was: 'it's those damned French again – lost their way.' He turned round and walked out of the door. He was right.

That was all to be in the future for me but the present political and military situation in Cairo in 1952 was enough to keep me busy. The Chief of the Imperial Staff, General Sir John Harding, met up with General Sir Brian Robertson, Commander of the Middle East Land Forces at GHQ in the Canal Zone. Although no formal communiqué was released, there was little doubt that the proposal for a Middle East Command to be established in Cyprus was discussed. *The Times* published a background piece from their 'Diplomatic Correspondent' which reviewed the concept since it had been first put forward as a Middle East Defence organisation when Nahas Pasha was in power; to no one's surprise it had been rejected.

Four powers were involved: the United States, France, and Turkey, led by the British Government. The proposition was to be put again to the Arab States and Israel. Cyprus was confirmed as a possible base for this new Command while accepting that nothing would adequately replace the Canal Zone as a Middle East base. Entering into these discussions, tentative though they were, Neguib at once threw a spanner into the works by calling on Prime Minister Ali Maher to hold a general election in February of the next year – effectively stalling any further talks on defence of the Middle East in which Egypt would be a partner. To soften the pill, Neguib, out of the blue, thanked the foreign residents for their support during the coup d'état, saying it was 'worthy of their nation's glorious part in securing the peace of the world'.[9] But Professor Hussein Kamel, Dean of Commerce of the University of Fayid, did not want to make any conciliatory remarks. He refuted strongly the conception that the Middle East was still a British sphere of influence, going on to say caustically, 'the tide was running strongly against Britain and she needed all her efforts to build up her own defences.' One has to assume that Sadat and Nasser, reading Neguib's eulogy of the mainly British residents' support and their possible future influence, inspired this quick response by a revolutionary academic.

However, despite the upheavals of the revolution, the diplomatic niceties continued with the re-accreditation of the British Ambassador, Sir Ralph Stevenson, in accordance with time honoured custom following a change of Monarchy. This involved new letters of credence from Her Majesty Queen Elizabeth to King Ahmed Fuad II, but significantly without any reference to his being King of Egypt and Sudan. The Regency, which had formed part of the Abdication statement, clearly calmed the immediate diplomatic waters, but it was not to last long.

Sadat's ill-concealed resentment of the respect given to Neguib by the Embassies in Cairo, not least our own, and their ready acceptance of him as both President and leader of the revolutionary movement, was mirrored by Nasser. Having used Neguib to bring it all about, with the firm intention of obtaining future political power, Nasser was indignant of the diplomatic sources which ignored the revolutionary junta. The final straw came from an article in *Life Magazine* in August 1952: 'The most militant and enterprising leader in Africa is Major-General Mohammed Neguib, Premier of Egypt. In the past nine months he has taken over a government, thrown out a king and made himself the idol of his people'.[10] Neguib's benign policy, in particular towards what Nasser viewed as the British occupying forces, was another irritation which could no longer be endured. This was not the climate of revolution which the Revolutionary Command Council had wanted to instil. The focus of press attention was now almost wholly concentrated on the political outcome of the coup d'état, with Neguib seemingly firmly entrenched. The diplomatic corps loved him. In the Canal Zone some 80,000 British and auxiliary forces maintained a wary presence. There were still incidents but nothing to compare with the Nahas era. Cairo life was returning to its old self-indulgent ways. But it was not to last.

In June 1953, coinciding with the month of the Coronation of Queen Elizabeth II, when the British press were writing reams about that and foreign news from Egypt and elsewhere was taking second place after nearly two years of capturing headlines, Nasser struck. His intention was to remove Neguib, but, again, with consummate skill, he would first remove old enemies of his brilliant coup of July 1952, and the challenge of the Moslem Brotherhood to create a state within a state.

The Brotherhood made an announcement of its religious aims: 'the realisation of the goals enjoyed by Islam, the clarification of the teaching of the Holy Koran and the true understanding of the

Moslem religion. Nasser saw this as a direct challenge to his vision of a new state combining the benefits of Western material civilisation with Islamic spiritual teaching; not the establishment of a pastoral theocracy based on the immutable teaching of the Koran, rejecting every aspect of alien culture, including its scientific and industrial achievements.'[11] He had also witnessed the destruction of Cairo in January 1952 and the targets selected by the Moslem Brotherhood for 'torching'. The Brotherhood's interpretation of the Koran, and their imposition of it, was alien to the section of the Moslem population of Egypt upon whose tolerance of other faiths and foreigners the prosperity of the nation depended.

So first Nasser scooped up Fuad Serag el Din, the clever propagandist, with a prison sentence of fifteen years. Then Madame Nahas, wife of the Wafd ex-Prime Minister Nahas Pasha, who had been associated with Serag el Din. It was common gossip, even when I arrived in Egypt in 1951, that between them they had cornered the cotton export market of that year, Egypt's foreign exchange holdings in one go. It was also gossip among my press contacts that Nahas Pasha had asked the then British Labour Government for a £50,000 loan on the grounds that 'wives will be wives'. The non-conformist labour administration was shocked and refused. Who knows, the gruff tolerance of Churchill, had he then been in power, might have saved the 1936 Treaty and all that had followed. Many thought Nahas Pasha's abrogation of the treaty was a deliberate diversion to avoid this becoming public knowledge.

These charges and severe sentences had been made by the Revolutionary Court and targeted other prominent figures including a member of the ex-royal family who was charged with profiteering during the Palestine War, many people close to Farouk, and a sprinkling of identifiable communists. None received the death sentence which was within the powers of the Court, but 'that the Court could impose the death sentence if it wished was all that was necessary for the public to see'.[12] This reluctance by Nasser to impose death sentences had been exemplified at the time of Farouk's abdication when, in long hours of debate by the junta, he fought to spare the King's life.

There remained the Moslem Brotherhood, a nettle Nasser would have to grasp before becoming, to all intents and purposes, the

Dictator of Egypt's future. He had no intention of sharing power with them after his next move which was to succeed Neguib as President. The Brotherhood had been disbanded in 1948 following the assassination of its then leader, Sheik Jassan el Banna. It had not, however, been proscribed, and even some members of the Council of Revolution were still closely associated with the 'Brothers' and their extreme attitude towards other faith communities in Egypt. Neguib and Sadat, on the other hand, had a sophisticated understanding of the roots of Islam and its relationship with other faiths, in particular Christianity. Neguib, as a young Captain in the army's Frontier Force, writing of a visit to Mount Sinai and St Catherine's Monastery with its icon of the Virgin Mary, put the theological position of Islam and Christianity as two monotheistic religions in words which might well be borne in mind today by followers of both faiths. He wrote: 'The Virgin Mary is revered by Moslems as well as Christians. Though we do not regard her as the Mother of God, or even as the Mother of the Son of God, we do regard her as the mother of the Prophet Jesus who was as close to God in his own way as the Prophet Mohammed was in his. I was therefore glad to join the priest in praying before her image.'[13] Later, as my family was leaving Cairo ahead of my eventual return to the War Office, Anwar Sadat came to my apartment with goodbye presents, giving Vivien, my eldest daughter, a silver brooch with an Arabic inscription which he translated for her as 'Praise be to God.' As we all said our goodbyes he said to me, 'I am Moslem and you are Christian but we both believe in the same God. I want you never to forget that'.

CHAPTER ELEVEN

The Downfall of Neguib

January 1954 gave Nasser the excuse he had been seeking when some twenty students were wounded in clashes between supporters of the University and the Moslem Brotherhood.[1] Moving quickly there was a round-up of 500 of the Brethren, their HQ was surrounded and their assets, amounting to £1 million sterling, were seized. There was to be a dreadful retribution in the future. On 6 October 1981, Anwar Sadat, having succeeded as President after Nasser's untimely death, was standing proudly in uniform on the Saluting Stand for the National Day military display, held every year to celebrate the victory over Israel in reclaiming Egyptian land. His wife was only a few feet behind him. An army truck which had joined, unnoticed, the column of artillery driving past, pulled out of the line. Closing in on the stand, its Islamic terrorists riddled Sadat with bullets. He died as Jehan struggled to reach his side, held back by her own bodyguard. By visiting Israel and seeking a peace pact, the radical element of the Brotherhood alleged he had betrayed Islam and declared it was 'the true Moslem's duty to set things straight, if not by words then by the Sword.'[2]

I had long since left the Middle East and the army, becoming the press attaché to the Archbishop of Canterbury in 1960. The shock of Anwar's death brought all my Cairo memories back, and this book is

Anwar and Jehan Sadat in October 1973 when Anwar was President.

much the result of retaining those memories and a dedication to him. I had recognised him when we first met as a man of great integrity, displaying all that is best in holding to Islam and the Koran, while tolerant and understanding of other faiths. It was this strength of purpose which had led him to seek conciliation with Israel, while never betraying his patriotic love of Egypt and his mission to bring the country out of domination by the British or any other nation. Had he lived, the world might never have seen the misery of the never ending conflict between Palestine and Israel, wreaking misery and war in the neighbouring countries. I grieved for Jehan who had so wonderfully supported him. One can only admire her for the worldwide recognition her book has achieved, and for her academic accomplishments as she sought to alleviate the miseries of those suffering from poverty and the extremes of some Islamic teaching and, above all, her fight on behalf of women for their the rightful place in the development of her country and its Arab neighbouring states.

By the end of 1953, however, with all that to come, I was soon to be on my way, posted back to the War Office once again, but not before I witnessed the early moves by Nasser to remove General Neguib. This was not easy as, by then, Neguib had established himself as a popular president and was carrying out some of the reforms which Sadat and Nasser had envisaged as young officers to change the course of Egyptian history. Nasser needed an excuse for reducing the power of the Moslem Brotherhood and getting rid of the 'hangers on' of discredited politicians of the old Wafd party. He had to deal with both. How was he to set about taking the final step of making himself virtual dictator of Egypt? It was a formidable task.

Neguib, during the halcyon days following the removal of Farouk, had not only been nominated as President, but also Prime Minister and President of the Revolutionary Command Council. Nasser himself gave way to the latter appointment, although the true position of Neguib was never more than that of 'primus inter pares' with the leaders of the Command Revolutionary Council. Nasser's tactics were, therefore, to erode Neguib's position of power by, as always, subtle moves that carried a message but avoided confrontation. First he received a Foreign Envoy on his own with no mention of it to Neguib, then he appointed three Cabinet Ministers, again without any reference to the 'President'.[3] An indignant Neguib demanded the right to veto new appointments as well as those just made. His protests were simply ignored. I was not to see the end of this internal battle before my return to England. In fact, it was not to come to a head until 25 February 1954, when Nasser pulled off another coup d'état, this time on Neguib whose graphic description of the morning it happened is recorded in his book published in 1955, only a year after his fall from power when the memories must have been fresh and painful. 'I awoke at 0630 hours. At 0700 hours after saying my prayers, I tried to call Farid [his Military Secretary] but my outside telephones were out of order. I tried my third and last line, a direct connection to the Command Council of Revolution. It was out of order. I realised I was under arrest.'4 Still living in his quite humble home, a barbed wire fence had been erected round the house area and was being patrolled by guards for his 'protection'. Sending his servant outside to see what was happening, he discovered that the guards had been replaced by regular army infantry and military police.

This had occurred only shortly before a planned visit to Sudan where Neguib had been invited to attend the inauguration of a Sudanese Provisional Government. It was an honour not only in Neguib's capacity as President, but also in recognition of his half Sudanese birth right. There then followed, in quick succession, two incidents reflecting the quasi-political moves which could only occur in what was still an unstable country emerging from a revolution. Cut off from any outside help, as he thought, in his besieged bungalow, he was awoken at 5.30 a.m., this time by a tapping on the window. Standing outside were two cavalry officers led by a Major Khalid Modi Din, the youngest member of the Command Revolution Council, who alleged that the Council had decided to make himself Prime Minister with Neguib continuing as President. It has to be said that Neguib took this with a pinch of salt. However, he played along with the two officers, suggesting that he would only remain as President if they and others were prepared to co-operate as 'comrades not Ministers'. It was enough to send them on their way rejoicing, declaring that a communiqué would be issued by the Council of Revolution announcing his terms, whereupon he would be driven to the HQ of the military government.

Khalid was only thirty-one. On his assurance to Neguib that he would remain as President of Egypt if he and his colleagues agreed to co-operate with him, Khalid departed from Neguib's home still in the early hours of the morning. But an unwelcome surprise in the shape of an angry Nasser, who had heard what was going on, met him on his way back to HQ. Khalid was later arrested, denounced as a communist and imprisoned.

Neguib did not remain at home for long. The next intervention on the same morning came from two military police officers who escorted him to a deserted area outside the artillery barracks at Almaza. Arriving there he was surrounded by a number of apparently angry young cavalry officers who, far from making an arrest, demanded that he remained as President, declaring that his recent visitors had been communist officers. Neguib, using his rank and long experience, calmed them down, even when they had driven him further into the desert to avoid any confrontation with Council of the Revolution forces stationed in the artillery barracks. Once again, Neguib found himself returned to his home, still surrounded by barbed wire. To add to this situation, a delegation from Sudan had arrived in Egypt declaring that this son of the Sudan and Egypt should be allowed to return with them if he was in danger, to retire in the Sudan if he wished.

Nasser had clearly miscalculated Neguib's popularity in the Services and the implications of his Sudanese birth. But once again, Nasser showed his ability to survive a political misfortune by issuing a proclamation that 'The Command Council of Revolution, in the name of the people, announces that the caravan will continue on its way with Mohammed Neguib in the van as President ... further that the Council headed by Gamal Abd el Nasser as Prime Minister, appeals to the Egyptian and Sudanese ... to restore tranquility.'[5] In one sentence Nasser had taken away Neguib's former title of 'President and Prime Minister', assuming the latter title for himself; it was to lead to Neguib's increased frustration and his threat to resign once again.

This time Nasser was more cautious and cunning before taking any action. Instigating three days of discussion, he offered to put Neguib in sole power as a resolution from the Command Council was put before an urgent meeting of the army Council. That meeting voted against the Council of Revolution's proposal to give way to Neguib, as Nasser had predicted. This gave him a green light, knowing he could now make his move for unquestioned power without interference from the army. Neguib accepted the inevitable and resigned from all his posts. His house was surrounded by an armed guard. The Council of Revolution met again through the night of 25 February. At 3 a.m. it was announced that Colonel Nasser had assumed full powers as chief of 'the ruling military junta, until the liberation of the country from Imperialistic forces'.[6] This was announced by Major Salah Salem, Minister for National Guidance, known to British readers as the 'dancing major'. Nasser had finally achieved the dictatorial powers he had always wanted. It also brought him to the attention of the world through extensive press coverage and the headlines denied to him when Neguib assumed power after the coup d'état. There were not one but two headlines with the same deadline:

GEN. NEGUIB RESIGNS
COLONEL NASSER IN CONTROL
3 AM MEETING

Cairo Feb 25th
President Neguib resigned all his Government posts. It was officially announced here today.

COL. NASSER IN FULL POWER
GEN NEGUIB UNDER ARMED GUARD

Cairo Feb 25th
The Council of the Revolution announced at 4.am today. In effect he has been divested of the presidency, the premiership and membership of the council.

Just who was this new Arab leader? Although known to the diplomatic community in Cairo, who reported on him to London, events in Egypt had been judged internationally until then on the actions of Neguib. The fact that he was a general who had served with the British army, albeit only for a few months towards the end of the desert war , had labelled him as a 'good chap'; certainly among British diplomats and service attachés he was considered 'one of us'. Nasser was anything but a friend of the British in Egypt. Although from a middle class background, he had had a chaotic school career. His mother died when he eight years old and he was put into the hands of successive relations in Egypt, while his father, a post office official, was transferred away from Cairo and married again, fathering ten children in all. Nasser ended up going to eight different schools; the last, when he was eighteen, was a hot bed for radical students and often mounted anti-British demonstrations. He had happily joined in and became friends with Anwar Sadat, a leading member, despite their very different social backgrounds. Both, however, had taken advantage of the opening of commissions in the army for all applicants – until then commissions had only been available to upper-class entrants. They therefore shared the same political views and formed an army comradeship from 1938 until 1941. Nasser had gone on to the Egyptian Staff College and Sadat to prison, but they remained firm friends; after all, both believed in ridding their army of corruption and their country of the British.

Sadat had paid heavily for his spying days in 1942 when Rommel was at the gates of Cairo. He was captured by no less than our 'Sammy', still the spy catcher and my rescuer from the Egyptian police.[7] The event itself reads like a script of the TV serial 'Allo Allo'. Two German agents wearing British uniforms driving a British staff car easily passed through the check points to the city. With £40,000 of Greek forged notes in their pockets, they hired a Nile houseboat, hid a transmitter and suborned themselves to the dubious delights of the Cairo night life. Drunk and distracted, with two ladies who had taken up residence on the boat, they failed to transmit very much. Questioned by their masters, they alleged that the transmitter had broken down. Sadat, just off a Signals course in the army and already a member of the revolutionary movement against the British occupation, was persuaded to fix it, but there was nothing wrong with it. One of the ladies on the boat was an intelligence contact for Sammy, who, of all things, was living in another Nile houseboat only two removed from the German agents. The agents started sobering up and saying nothing. Then, to add to this strange tale, Winston Churchill was meeting General Slim and King Farouk in Cairo on his way to the Moscow Conference of 1942 and demanded to question the agents himself. He promised to save their lives if they talked, which they did, leading to the arrest of Anwar Sadat. Churchill will have remembered his name which gives credence to the rumour that he intervened in his prison sentence to ameliorate his conditions – a fact which I believe played a part in Anwar's friendship with me. Coming out of prison, Anwar was at Nasser's side from then on to achieve Neguib's downfall and defeat any opposition party that might still be a political threat.

Nasser had set about discrediting Neguib's reputation before driving him to resignation. He did this by secretly releasing the Nahas government politicians from their prisons, including Nahas Pasha himself, and let it be known that it was Neguib who had imprisoned them. As Premier, Nasser had lifted press censorship so his actions would give rise to international and local press coverage. He also alleged that Neguib had planned to disband the Revolutionary Council. This, helped by the usual 'rent-a-crowd', enraged the fellahin to riot in the streets and accuse Neguib of being a traitor to the revolution. Just as Nasser had planned, public opinion was stirred up and Neguib was portrayed as a dictatorial General, the opposite of his real character and actions during his time as President. In their statement following Neguib's resignation, the officers of the Revolutionary Council accepted Lieutenant-Colonel Nasser as 'having assumed full powers as Chief of the ruling military junta until the liberation of the country from imperialist forces.'

It was also important for Nasser to consolidate his position to justify his actions to the Sudanese. He was aware of the delegation from Sudan which had arrived by chance on the day of Neguib's arrest. In the event, Nasser's plans worked out well following the mayhem and demonstrations which had been organised in the streets against Neguib. In an even more subtle move, the Revolutionary Council, while the mayhem was going on, indicated that it would not accept his resignation. 'We' they said blandly, 'will govern in your name.' As soon as they announced this the strikes ceased and calm returned to the streets! Nasser had accomplished what he wanted – international recognition that he was the true leader of the revolution. He immediately reformed his cabinet establishing himself firmly as Prime Minister, and appointed, *inter alia*, Anwar Sadat as a Minister of State who had done so much to support Nasser as editor of the influential *El Gurihuria*. Anwar remained as a Director in an even more powerful position to influence Egyptian public opinion in favour of Nasser. Neguib became a sick man and, although remaining as President for two months following his arrest and reinstatement, he finally resigned and retired for the last time. He was heard of no more, retiring to a modest dwelling some distance from Cairo. But before that he had had to suffer a final indignity. In November 1954, when there was an abortive attempt by the Moslem Brotherhood to assassinate Nasser, who could be the inspiration but Neguib? His house was surrounded once again and he was taken to a suburb of Cairo, where, according to some accounts, he could have been murdered. But once again his Sudanese heritage came to his rescue with the Sudan Government intervening and offering him refuge to face down any further attempt at humiliation. He was at last left in peace.

Nasser was now finally President. His overwhelming ambitions were eventually to lead him into conflict with Britain, France, and Israel through his nationalisation of the Suez Canal, the invasion of Port Said and Suez, the humiliating withdrawal of British forces, and the political demise of Prime Minister Anthony Eden.

Neguib, by virtue of his military background in the tradition of the British army, was not cut out to be a politician. He had entered into Middle East politics as the face of Sadat and Nasser, who had been nurtured by their long political involvement in Egyptian affairs. He had little chance of succeeding in the long term. In fact, he had been used and finally he knew it. But, in one respect, he had played an important role in bringing about the eventual independence of the Sudan. On 12 February 1953, almost a year before the demise of his career, a new 'Agreement' had been signed replacing that aspect of the Anglo-Egyptian 1936 Treaty which had linked Sudan to Egypt through a joint sovereignty: a 'condominium between the King of Egypt and the reigning Monarch of Great Britain, represented by a Governor General.' Clearly the time had come for reform.

To enable the Sudanese to determine their own future, a three year period of transition was established to bring to an end any link between the Sudan and Egypt through the Anglo-Egyptian Treaty and its hated condominium clause. The British appointed Governor General of Sudan would be replaced by a 'Supreme Constitutional Authority'. The most difficult problem facing the Commission entrusted with reforming the constitution was to be its membership.

At the end of the day it was comprised of two Sudanese, one
Egyptian, a Pakistani and, last but not least, a Briton. Neguib was
well placed to see this through. His maternal grandfather and three
of his brothers had been killed in the defence of Khartoum during the
uprising of the Mahadi which led to the death of General Gordon.
Neguib's father and uncle had later been Egyptian army officers. The
relief force, led by General Kitchener, had stirred the imagination of
colonial observers throughout the Empire, and its place in history was
sealed by Winston Churchill's account as a young officer in the 21st
Lancers, taking part in the last cavalry charge of the British army.[8]
Writing in the same book towards the end of his time in the Sudan,
he likens the Nile to a palm tree, with its roots in Egypt and the vast
bend, flowing south of Khartoum, where the 'roots of the tree begin
to stretch deeply into the Soudam [sic]. Water – the life – of the Delta
is drawn from the Soudam [sic] and passes along the channel of
the Nile as the sap passes up the stem of the tree, to produce a fine
crop of fruit above.' Enlarging on the metaphor, he concludes with
uncanny prescience, 'of what use would be the roots and the rich soil
if the stem were severed'. The misery of Sudan, as it developed into
an independent self-governing country, is highlighted by the tragedy
of Darfur, an enormous region, twice the size of Egypt with half its
population.[9] There, at the time of writing, the death toll is reaching
some 500,000 through starvation and inter-tribal massacres. This
can only cause one to reflect on the peace and harmony that ruled the
region during the colonial years.

   The early signs of dissension and violence met Neguib as he arrived
in Sudan. There had been a rebellion in the south at the inauguration
ceremonies, with a riot resulting in the death of twenty-two Sudanese
and the British Chief of Police. Following these riots in Khartoum,
Harold Macmillan, writing only a year later also with prescience
following further riots in the south of Sudan (now Darfur), observed
that, 'the people are of a quite different race and character protesting
against northern domination. The rising was put down after much
slaughter, but it was an evil omen for the future'.[10]

   Whisked away in a blacked out Government car, Neguib was driven
to the 'Palace' of the still Governor General, Sir Robert Howe. He
was unable to contact the leader of the Umma party leading the riot,
whom he knew and hoped to help quell the situation. Instead, he was

confined to try to deal through intermediaries. Frustrated, Neguib left within three days. Writing of this, he recalls his meeting with Selwyn Lloyd, the Minister of State sent from Britain to represent HMG. 'He warned me to be careful lest I was killed. I expressed my opinion that as a Briton, his life was in greater danger than mine.'[11] The subsequent history of this once prosperous colony, the breadbasket of that region of central Africa, is sadly the story of so many nations once embraced by the British Empire in its heyday, and administered by a dedicated Colonial Service. Although hardly ever mentioned and certainly not taught today within any school history curriculum, 'Pax Britannica', backed by armed force when necessary, once ruled over 23 per cent of the world's population, covering 20 per cent of the earth's surface.[12] Sudan in the 1920s was recognised as one of the most sought after posts by young Colonial Service officers, many graduates of Oxbridge. It was where the paternalistic ethos of that service had flourished. Armed force was then at its minimum. Indeed, I had reported to the press in Cairo the move of just one infantry Battalion from Suez as a reinforcement following the abrogation of the 1936 Treaty and Sudanese condominium.

At the end of the day, Harold Macmillan, taking one of his last actions as Foreign Secretary before becoming Chancellor of the Exchequer, was to press for immediate self-government for the Sudan before awaiting the conclusion of the Constituent Assembly period. Neguib returned to Cairo to meet his fate.

Col. Hornby

LISTE

DE M.M. LES MEMBRES

DU

CORPS DIPLOMATIQUE

Juillet 1952

GRANDE-BRETAGNE *(suite)*

16, Rue El Amir Fouad, Zamalek.	**M. le Lieut-Colonel R.J.A. Hornby,** *Attaché Militaire Adjoint.* **Mme. Hornby.**	30 Nov. 1951
14, Rue El Saraya el Koubra Garden City. **Tél. 56657**	**M. le Major Cyril Philip Tamlyn,** *Attaché Militaire Adjoint.*	16 Juin 1951
4, Rue Mohamed Mazhar Pacha, Zamalek. **Tél. 78262**	**M. le Sqd./Leader K. Johnson,** *Attaché de l'Air Adjoint.*	12 Mars 1951
4, Rue Mohamed Mazhar Pacha, Zamalek. **Tél. 51434**	**M. K.H. Clucas,** *2ème Secrétaire (Affaires Ouvrières),*	12 Oct. 1950
10, Rue Saraya el Guézireh, Zamalek. **Tél. 58690**	**M. J.G. Tomlinson,** *2ème. Secrétaire.* **Mme. Tomlinson.**	19 Août 1946
Cornwall Court. 6, Rue El Aziz Osman, Zamalek. **Tél. 47729**	**M. W.F.H. Robiou,** *2ème. Secrétaire (Affaires Consulaires).* **M. Robiou.**	18 Avril 1950

— 40 —

Extract from the list of British diplomats living in Cairo in 1952, published by the Ministère Royal des Affaires Étrangères.

CHAPTER TWELVE

Swan Song

At the beginning of 1953, I was still in Cairo and still despatching copy from the Canal Zone to London. This was to provoke a confrontation with the established foreign correspondents and news agency offices based in Cairo. During the attacks on the British army in 1951 and 1952, with severe censorship imposed on copy sent through Cable and Wireless, my clandestine operations were approved by the Embassy, the army in the Canal Zone, the War Office and, with gratitude, by Cairo based correspondents subjected to censorship. It depended on every correspondent keeping to the code not to reveal how their detailed despatches of the persistent attacks on British troops were being submitted to the world press. The only exemption was for War Office approved journalists visiting Fayid in the Canal Zone to write up the role of the British forces. These were mainly reporters from provincial papers doing 'local boy' stories. There were exceptions involving the national press which I was soon to find out.

Egyptian press censorship had been imposed since the abrogation of the 1936 Treaty during the attacks made on British forces, and was now being extended for periods under Neguib. However, internal political conflicts following the Abdication and the emergence of the Command Revolutionary Council raised the question of whether it was still right to evade censorship when no British forces in the Canal Zone were involved.

The issue came to a head when, on the night of 16 January 1953, twenty-five Egyptian army officers were arrested for planning a coup against Neguib, President of Egypt. This was headline stuff: 'ARMY OFFICERS ARRESTED IN EGYPTIAN PLOT. ALL POLITICAL PARTIES DISSOLVED BY GENERAL NEGUIB.' Thus ran the Reuters report in *The Times* headline of 17 January, followed by an extensive résumé, broadcast by the 'Minister for National Guidance', of the aims of the military movement and reasons for these arrests. This is worth quoting from *The Times* for the sting in its tail.

'The first aim of the revolutionary movement,' this new Minister said, 'was the evacuation of foreign forces from the land. We are now about to realise this supreme aim whatever might be the circumstances and obstacles. We expect the political parties to appreciate the high interests of the Nation and to abandon the destructive methods of partisanship detrimental to the Country.'

The first journalist to contact me was Sidney Rodin of the *Sunday Express*, who came into my office on Saturday afternoon on 17 January 1953 asking to use my 'telephone service'. As there had been no restrictions on it, as I thought at the time, I telephoned it through and was also able to inform the Embassy of the details of his despatch. As a result of my call, Rodin got a scoop in the *London Sunday Express*, leaving the Cairo press correspondents behind in sending full coverage and local reaction. Colin Reid of the *Telegraph*, no doubt chased by his news editor in London, defended himself for being scooped and cabled back: 'this was all Colonel Hornby's fault for giving Rodin a scoop and blocking the Cairo correspondents.' To make matters worse, Pawley, the managing editor of the *Telegraph* and their military correspondent, General Martin, sent messages through the Egyptian censor direct to Reid in Cairo and to GHQ Fayid, thus compromising all the Cairo press. Reid was instructed to send his despatch either through my link or direct from the Canal Zone. He then gave me his copy on the evening of the 18th and, to play an even hand with Rodin, unaware of the furore, I sent it. Not content with that, Reid also sent another report and more background to GHQ Fayid for onward transmission to the *Telegraph* in London, using Royal Signals by hand of a messenger he knew in Cairo. That story was blocked by Colonel Carroll, the Director of Public Relation Middle East Command. By then I knew of the decision of the correspondents, including Reid and Rodin, who had met among themselves; they had decided they should abide by the rules of the country and comply with censorship when they were reporting political events which did not affect the security or lives of the army personnel outside the Egyptian Government's writ. As they had not told me that it would apply to the events of 17 January and the coup d'état against Neguib, I had felt free to use my clandestine means of avoiding Egyptian censorship if I was asked to do so by an established journalist and it was in the interests of helping the press. It was to lead to my one and only confrontation with the Cairo based foreign correspondents, and more importantly the five news agencies on whom the press then relied so much for background and 'news flashes'.

What I did learn, never to forget, in my subsequent dealings with the newspaper world was the intense competition between newspapers seeking readership and therefore sales in their chosen market. This in turn determines the advertising rates they could command. It is as though the circulation figures and the revenue from advertising are joined by an umbilical cord, each feeding from the other. The role of the foreign correspondent and, indeed, other specialist writers is to generate the news behind the headlines which will grab the readers' attention. Colin Reid's perennial question, 'have you filed yet?' said it all. As did Ralph Izzard's reply on one occasion when I was also among them, 'No, cannot find a story,' when he had on that morning located an Italian tanker carrying oil to Israel breaking the blockade, scooping all the rest of the journalists. This was the game played between journalists to keep their jobs. Some two weeks later, I received long letters from Tom Little, the doyen of the Cairo press, and Tom Clayton of the *Daily Express*. They set out the reasons for their decision not to evade Egyptian censorship over Cairo based political news. They are such revealing letters – thoughtful, and, in their way, erudite – that I reproduce them in Appendices 2 and 3. The meeting they describe runs counter, of course, to all the canons of journalism, and I doubt whether any of my friends would have admitted consenting to such an agreement. On the other hand, both Colin Reid and Sidney Rodin had been at the meeting and had deliberately scooped their competitors. The role of a 'spokesman' is not an easy one! More interesting is the basic camaraderie between correspondents reporting from dangerous missions which resulted in Reid being allowed back into the fold. Eventually he came to see me in my flat explaining all that had happened and was clearly quite upset at what he had done. We had been good friends and remained so. It was a different matter with Rodin. He had only been a 'visiting fireman', spending a few days between Cairo and the Canal Zone, and had returned to London almost immediately after asking me to avoid Egyptian censorship when he could have handed it straight to his office in London and still caught the later Sunday edition of his paper. The fact that Tom Clayton is critical of Rodin in his letter, a fellow journalist in the same group, shows that he went too far in testing the ultimate goodwill of his fellow journalists. He never came back to Cairo while I was there!

The attention of the press in 1953 continued to be focused on Cairo, but the number of correspondents was dropping off and those who wanted to use me as a spokesman or arrange visits to the Canal Zone was also less than during the hectic days of 1952, with its burnings of Cairo, abdication of Farouk, and the political and military upheavals of the new regime. So when invited to one of the press watering holes I would usually accept a round or two of drinks and chat. I was at the Metropole, one of their favourites, with Ralph Izzard and Colin Reid when the familiar sight of a small turbaned boy with a red coat clutching a telegram for Ralph appeared at the swing door. Ralph held out his hand and put his telegram on the bar as if it was of no interest. Colin immediately asked 'from the office?' 'Oh I will have a look', said Ralph and he did so, carefully screening it from Colin. Not a muscle moved on his face as he took a quick sip from his glass and put it back on the bar. We talked a little longer and, as Colin slid off the bar stool ready to go, Ralph put the telegram in front of me, still sitting at the bar, so that Colin could not see it. It was in the standard cablese of the day: 'Proceed soonest Kathmandu. Essential you secure room best hotel for view final assault Everest'. There then followed detailed advice on where in Cairo to obtain mountaineering equipment boots and much else! We had all by then known of the proposed final assault to reach the top of Everest by an expedition led by Sir John Hunt and the Sherpa Tensing. What the London press also knew was that *The Times* had obtained exclusive rights for press coverage against the expedition's costs. The message to Ralph was clear – break *The Times* exclusive. The world also knew that Princess Elizabeth was to be crowned on 3 June. Would John Hunt be successful before the Coronation? He was almost to the day. The headline in the *Express*, written by its then editor, Edward Pickering, later Sir Edward and Rupert Murdoch's right hand man in London, said it all on the morning of the Coronation: 'ALL THIS AND EVEREST TOO.'

The *Daily Mail* was not far behind with a front page picture of its 'intrepid' reporter who had climbed to first base and was being welcomed with open arms by the expedition's doctor. Ralph had given up his hotel room for a 100 mile trek to the mountain. Actually, Ralph told me when I met him again in London, the 'welcoming arms' in the photograph were the expedition's doctor trying to shoo him off the mountain as he was fearful of upsetting the *The Times*. They were right to be careful. Ralph Izzard was taking on *The Times* correspondent, Jan Morris, who indeed viewed the final assault graphically described in her book 'Coronation Everest'. I had met her in Cairo where she was reporting as 'James', but her 'new life' brought her fame and the authorship of some thirty books describing her many adventurous assignments for *The Times* and other papers, culminating in being awarded a well deserved CBE Ralph never really got beyond Base Camp, but that was high enough for the expedition doctor. After they became friends, the doctor warned him about lack of oxygen and that he should have been wearing a mask. I remember Ralph telling me that his reply was 'Doctor! If you had spent as long as I have in smoke filled night clubs you would not need your mask for lack of oxygen!'

Egypt and the desert road from Heliopolis to Fayid were to leave me with one final memory. As it is the army custom to get rid of families as soon as may be, although I was being posted back to the War Office I would have to remain alone in Cairo until my replacement could be found. My wife was given the choice to stay over Christmas without the children or to go home. The choice was obvious! So packing the baggage and two children I drove once again down the desert road in my new car, a Triumph Herald I had just bought and had serviced at the English-run garage in Cairo. All

The author in uniform having received an OBE at GHQ Fayid.

went well and the family embarked on Her Majesty's troop ship, the *Empire Windrush*. It was just as well that I knew nothing about it then, but a year later on 28 March 1954 it caught fire with 1,700 men and women on board, capturing world headlines. Like the *Empire Ken* on which we had, as a family, 'trooped' to Mombasa, it was a previous German ship captured by British troops at Kiel in 1945. This time they had managed to get it intact unlike the *Empire Ken* with its fifteen degree list which the German Captain managed to create by sabotage just before being captured. Like the *Empire Ken* too the *Windrush* had been allocated to the German SS. Whether there was still some malign influence, my wife had a serious problem with our younger daughter who was diagnosed by the ship's doctor with an incipient appendicitis. There were very limited medical facilities on board, but all turned out well in the end. It was typical, in its day, of the stress which so many army wives and children suffered 'following the drum'.

For my part, driving back alone and feeling a bit down, the engine suddenly made the noise all motorists dread – rattles, bangs and a full stop. I was fifty odd miles from Cairo and all around me was the familiar desert. No mobile phones in those days! I waited a very long time but eventually was picked up by a passing army jeep. What followed was a long tow rope to the Heliopolis border post, frantic calls for someone to find Tantawi, and the bright blue army vanguard. A few days later the mystery was solved. A mechanic, through malice or just carelessness, had left a large oily rag in the oil sump. It had cleaned the oil beautifully drifting round Cairo, but high speed and heat was too much and the engine had seized up. There then came another long tow – this time behind Tantawi – driving to Alexandria to catch a freighter for the Port of London. My last memorable sight in this ancient city where so much had happened while I had been in Egypt was of my pride and joy being hoisted onto an open deck, not knowing when or in what condition I would see it again.

Detail from picture on p. 97.

Epilogue

In 1954, President Abdul Nasser assured Eden, then Foreign Secretary, that if British forces evacuated the Canal Zone there would be an end to hostile action. Eden's acceptance of this promise was to have fatal consequences. In July 1956, Nasser declared his intention to nationalise the Suez Canal, which was jointly owned by Britain and France. It was a humiliation Eden was not prepared to accept. His reputation as statesman was at stake. Moreover, Russia had become Egypt's ally and paymaster – allowing Nasser to nationalise the Suez Canal would give control of a vital international waterway to an unfriendly power. Eden had to restore his authority at home and abroad.

A re-invasion of the Egyptian territories bordering the Canal was the only course of action as he saw it. But this was also politically unacceptable. Eden needed a viable reason for military action, and how he achieved this was kept a secret for many years. His solution was to proclaim that Israel was about to attack Egypt, and that British forces would land in Egypt again to 'protect' British interests. In fact, Israel's planned invasion was a collusion between France, Israel, and Britain, of whom only the latter had any intention of attacking Egypt. A secret meeting was held at Sèvres in France between the French Prime Minister, accompanied by defence and foreign ministers, and

Israel's Prime Minister and Chief of Staff. Eden was represented by his Foreign Secretary, Selwyn Lloyd, and a very senior diplomat, Sir Donald Logan, whose task was to ensure that all the documents were destroyed at the end of the meeting, in particular those relating to HMG participation.

I am indebted to *The Times* obituary on the death of Sir Donald, published on 5 November 2009, for drawing attention to an article written by him and published in the *The Financial Times* on 2 January 1986 entitled 'Collusion at Suez'. Surprisingly, Logan's article appears to have attracted little attention at the time, but much of this has resulted since in articles and on TV programmes.

On 31st October [1956], with RAF aircraft already pounding Egypt, a Royal Navy Task Force left Malta comprised of H.M.S. *Eagle*, H.M.S. *Albion* and H.M.S. *Bulwark* carrying Fleet Air Arm aircraft and H.M.S. *Ocean* and H.M.S. *Theseus* carrying helicopters and troops bound for the beaches. The LST Lofoten, with men and equipment of No.45 Commando onboard, also accompanied the fleet with its escort of destroyers and frigates. Meanwhile, the cruiser H.M.S. *Newfoundland* encountered an unknown contact while on patrol at the southern end of the canal zone. The target, on being challenged, opened fire on the cruiser causing minor damage. The Newfoundland replied with her 6 inch guns and sunk the Egyptian frigate *Domiat* after six minutes, 69 of her crew being rescued.

At 4.44 am on 5th November, six hundred men of 3 Para were dropped from RAF Hasting and Valetta aircraft onto El Gamil airfield. They soon secured the airfield against little opposition and achieved all their objectives during the day, and were reinforced when another drop of 100 men and equipment was made in the afternoon.

The Seaborne landings the following morning were at Port Said and the French held Port Fuad. Nos. 40 and 42 Commando was flown ashore by Six Whirlwinds and Six Sycamore helicopters from H.M.S. *Ocean* and Whirlwinds from H.M.S. *Theseus*, landing virtually unopposed, although a few pockets of determined resistance were dealt with by the Close Air Support which was always present.

By the end of the day, the Allied forces had consolidated their positions and were confident that the Suez Canal would be in their hands within the next 24 hours. During the night the first LSTs berthed at Port Said and began unloading their Centurion tanks. At that point, the Allies were forced to withdraw under pressure from the United Nations and Russia, a Ceasefire coming into effect on 2345 on 6th November. The troops began to evacuate on 7th December and the last troops left on 22nd December.

It was all to no avail. Faced by a hostile United Nations and Russia, Eden succumbed to political pressure and withdrew his forces on 22 December 1956 to the new Middle East base in Cyprus. Eden resigned as Prime Minister on grounds of ill health on 9 November 1957.

A British soldier guarding a street in Ismailia, January 1952. (*Mirrorpix*)

References

Prologue
  1. Artemis Cooper, *Cairo in the War*, Hamish Hamilton, 1985

Chapter One
  1. *Reader's Digest Great World Atlas*
  2. Elspeth Huxley, *Nine Faces of Kenya*, Collins Harvill, 1990

Chapter Two
Nil

Chapter Three
  1. *The Times*, 6 October 1951
  2. *The Times*, 11 October 1951
  3. *The Times*, 11 October 1951
  4. *The Times*, 20 October 1951

Chapter Four
  1. Alfred Sansom, *I Spied Spies*, Harrap & Co., 1965

Chapter Five
1. *The Times*, 13 November 1952
2. *The Times*, 3 December 1952
3. *The Times*, 13 December 1952
4. *The Times*, 27 December 1952
5. *The Times*, 9 January 1952

Chapter Six
1. *The Times*, 21st January 1952
2. *The Times*, 24th January 1952

Chapter Seven
1. Anwar Sadat, *Revolt on the Nile*, Allan Wingate, 1957
2. Jehan Sadat, *Woman of Egypt*, Bloomsbury Publishing, 1987
3. Jehan Sadat, *Woman of Egypt*, Bloomsbury Publishing, 1987
4. Max Rodenbeck, *Cairo, The City Victorious*, Picador, 1988
5. Barrie St Clair McBride, *Farouk of Egypt*, Robert Hale, 1967
6. Sir Ralph Stevenson, *Report to the Foreign Office*, 20 November 1952
7. Jehan Sedat, *Woman of Egypt*, Bloomsbury Publishing, 1987
8. Jehan Sedat, *Woman of Egypt*, Bloomsbury Publishing, 1987
9. Jehan Sedat, *Woman of Egypt*, Bloomsbury Publishing, 1987
10. *The Times*, 14 February 1952
11. *The Times*, 25 February 1952

Chapter Eight
Nil

Chapter Nine
1. Tom Little, *Egypt*, Ernest Benn, 1958
2. Anwar Sadat, *Revolt on the Nile*, Allan Wingate, 1957
3. Alfred Sansom, *I Spied Spies*, Harrap & Co., 1965
4. Anwar Sadat, *Revolt on the Nile*, Allan Wingate, 1957
5. Anwar Sadat, *Revolt on the Nile*, Allan Wingate, 1957
6. Mohammed Hercal, *Nasser – The Cairo Documents*, New English Library
7. Jehan Sadat, *Woman of Egypt*, Bloomsbury Publishing, 1987
8. Jehan Sadat, *Woman of Egypt*, Bloomsbury Publishing, 1987

9. Jehan Sadat, *Woman of Egypt*, Bloomsbury Publishing, 1987
10. Jehan Sadat, *Woman of Egypt*, Bloomsbury Publishing, 1987

Chapter Ten
  1. Mohammed Neguib, *Egypt's Destiny*, Victor Gollancz, 1955
  2. Anwar Sadat, *In Search of Identity*, Harper Row, 1977
  3. Jehan Sadat, *Woman of Egypt*, Bloomsbury Publishing, 1987
  4. Anwar Sadat, *In Search of Identity*, Harper Row, 1977
  5. Jehan Sadat, *Woman of Egypt*, Bloomsbury Publishing, 1987
  6. Alfred Sansom, *I Spied Spies*, Harrap & Co.,1965
  7. Jehan Sadat, *Woman of Egypt*, Bloomsbury Publishing, 1987
  8. Barrie St Clare McBride, *Farouk of Egypt*, Victor Gollancz, 1967
  9. Mohammed Neguib, *Egypt's Destiny*, Victor Gollancz, 1955
  10. *Life Magazine*, August 1952
  11. Joachim Joeston, *Nasser, The Rise to Power*, Odham's Press Ltd, 1960
  12. Joachim Joeston, *Nasser, The Rise to Power*, Odham's Press Ltd, 1960
  13. Mohammed Neguib, *Egypt's Destiny*, Victor Gollancz, 1955

Chapter Eleven
  1. Joachim Joeston, *Nasser, The Rise to Power*, Odham's Press Ltd, 1960
  2. Max Rodenbeck, *Cairo, The City Victorious*, Picador, 1988
  3. Joachim Joeston, *Nasser, The Rise to Power*, Odham's Press Ltd, 1960
  4. Mohammed Neguib, *Egypt's Destiny*, Victor Gollancz, 1955
  5. Joachim Joeston, *Nasser, The Rise to Power*, Odham's Press Ltd, 1960
  6. *The Times*, 25 February 1954
  7. Alfred Sansom, *I Spied Spies*, Harrap & Co., 1965
  8. Winston Churchill, *The River War*, Eyre & Spottiswoode, 1933
  9. British Empire and Commonwealth Museum, Bristol
  10. Harold Macmillan, *Tide of Fortune 1945-1955*, Thomson Newspapers
  11. Mohammed Neguib, *Egypt's Destiny*, Victor Gollancz, 1955
  12. British Empire and Commonwealth Museum, Bristol

The author in dress uniform on his retirement from the army in 1962.

Appendices

APPENDIX ONE

The Abdication Document put before King Farouk at Ras al Tin Palace, Alexandria, at 12.30 p.m. on 25 July 1952, requiring his departure from Egypt aboard the royal yacht by six o'clock the same evening.

Although the document included a provision for Crown Prince Fuad II to succeed him, neither the deposed King, his son, nor any member of his close family were ever to set foot in Egypt again.

To the Egyptian people: My fellow countrymen. To complete the work which your valiant Army has undertaken for your cause, I [General Neguib Bey, Commander in Chief of the Armed Forces] met today Ali Maher, the Egyptian Prime Minister, and handed him a petition directed to His Majesty Farouk I, containing two demands from the people: first to abdicate in favour of his Highness, the Crown Prince, before noon today: and second to leave the Country before six o'clock today. His Majesty graciously agreed to the two demands which were carried into effect at the appointed times without any untoward incident.

Our success in the country's cause is due first and last to your solidarity with us, to the strict manner in which you have carried out our directives and to the fact that you have maintained tranquility. I am quite aware that you have been overjoyed, therefore appeal to you to continue to maintain your self restraint in order that we may carry out your country's cause to a successful conclusion. We are confident that you will follow such directives for the sake of the fatherland and the welfare and prosperity of the people.

The royal prescript complied with all the army's demands.

> We, Farouk, King of Egypt and the Sudan: Since we always seek the welfare of our Nation, its happiness and advancement and since we certainly desire our country to overcome the difficulties which it is facing in the present delicate circumstances and in compliance with the wishes of the people, we have decided to abdicate in favour of our son, Crown Prince Ahmed Fuad. We have issued orders to his Excellency Ali Maher Pasha, President of the Council of Ministers, to act in accordance therewith.

The final act was an announcement by this Council proclaiming His Majesty Ahmed Fuad II as King of Egypt and the Sudan, beseeching the Almighty that the country may enjoy during his reign the development, glory and happiness to which it is looking forward.

APPENDIX TWO

Letter from T. R. (Tom) Little, General Manager Arab News Agency, Egypt, correspondent for the *Observer* newspaper, the *Economist*, and deputy correspondent of *The Times* (Middle East).

February 5, 1953

Col. Robert Hornby,
British Embassy,
Cairo.

Dear Colonel Hornby,

In view of the discussions which have been going on here among the journalists about the use of the radio communication facilities in the Canal Zone, I am taking the liberty of giving you my opinion on the subject. I do so because I think I have the right to do so as General Manager of the Arab News Agency, correspondent of 'The Economist' and 'The Observer' and Deputy Correspondent of 'The Times' in the Middle East and because I believe there has been much woolly talk about the subject at issue. However, I am expressing my personal views as a resident journalist and not those of any of the firms for which I write. I am personally convinced that they would be in complete agreement with me.

1. In my opinion the British Army is not entitled to break the censorship laws of Egypt in normal circumstances, because Britain has officially denied the abrogation of the 1936 Treaty. H.M.G. having taken up this position, the Army has no right to base a breach of Egypt's laws and decrees on Egypt's claim to have abrogated the Treaty. In more general terms, we are not justified in treating Egypt as an enemy as long as the two countries have engaged on new talks for an amicable settlement.

2. From this position, it follows that the circumstances in which the Canal Zone facilities are granted to journalists are those in which Egypt adopts a policy which is contrary to our treaty claims and prevents the correspondents by censorship from conveying a true picture of the situation to Britain. In other words, the Egyptian action must either endanger or threaten to endanger the rights and/or safety of the British troops or the British civil population.

3. One might stretch a point to allow news to be sent out direct from the Canal Zone regarding the troops and their conditions, although there is not the slightest reason why the usual facilities offered by Marconi should not be used. Clearly there is no secret involved if the material is intended for publication in the newspapers.

4. On no account should the Canal Zone facilities be used: a) in such a way as to threaten the stability of the Egyptian Government which is officially that of a friendly Power; or b) in such a way as to endanger the future use of those facilities in times of crisis when the rights and/or safety of Britons in Egypt are challenged. It would be most unfortunate for example, if as a result of the abuse of the Zone facilities now, journalists were prevented from traveling on the Cairo-Fayid road during a crisis in order to prevent their using the facilities.

5. In my opinion, the stories sent out by the Canal Zone on behalf of Rodin of the Sunday Express and Noyes Thomas of the News of the World contravened what should be the 'correct rules' for using the Canal Zone facilities.

Rodin, who was making a brief visit to Cairo, found himself obstructed by censorship and asked for facilities in the Canal Zone and I do not think he can be held blameworthy since it was his duty as a journalist to use what facilities lay to hand. Other journalists, notably Thomas Clayton and Douglas Howell of the Daily Express and Daily Mirror respectively consulted me and I said that the Canal Zone facilities were not available for such stories as an attempted coup d'etat against the Government of a friendly Power and, rely on my experience here, they did not attempt to use them. Neither did Colin Reid of the Daily Telegraph nor Ralph Izzard of the Daily Mail at this stage.

But: my advice would have been very different if I had known that Noyes Thomas and Mc Whinney (of the Daily Herald) were in the Canal Zone at the invitation of the British Army. The Army signals in the Canal Zone sent out a message, which presumably had been approved by the Army PRO there, which was completely false in its picture of the conditions in Egypt in that it gave a grossly false sense of military emergency. By comparison, Rodin's story, colourfully inaccurate, of the events taking place in Cairo, was harmless.

6. I would say most emphatically that journalists who are brought out on visits by the British Forces to do stories about the conditions in the Canal Zone should be limited to those stories and not allowed to write about situations of which they, not having strayed from the Canal Zone, have absolutely no knowledge except mess gossip and military briefing. There is not reason why the Forces should not pay for journalists to come out on visas in the normal way and leave them to use the normal, commercial communications while here; but if for P.R.O. purposes the Forces desire to send out correspondents, then it should be clearly laid down in advance that while in the Canal Zone the communications there can only be used for stories concerning the conditions of the troops and that they must go outside the camp to file through normal commercial channels stories which concern the situation in civilian Egypt.

7. Unless the Army Command makes a rule of this sort, it is extremely difficult to refuse similar facilities to any visiting or resident British correspondent. For that reason I think it was impossible to refuse Rodin facilities on the weekend in question, although I think it was basically wrong to grant them.

8. I would like to point out most strongly that the offer of facilities to journalists in almost any conditions does harm to the resident correspondents who endanger their whole position in the country if they are proved guilty of using army communications. This means, in effect, that the visiting journalist who spends a few days in the country and frequently knows nothing of the situation and who has no stake or interest in the continuing evolution of the situation, is able to 'scoop' his better-informed colleagues with sensational stories which, in the nature of things, are almost certain to be inaccurate and are frequently damaging to Britain as much as to Egypt.

9. In conversations among the correspondents after the week-end in question, ideas such as those outlined very fully above gave rise to the request that facilities should not be granted under those conditions.

I would emphasise that no responsible journalists asks that facilities should be completely denied. The value of the Canal Zone communications in the Autumn of 1951 is beyond question and there might be other circumstances in which they would again be vital. What the journalists do say is that there should be some clear conception of the conditions under which the facilities will be granted and that, in general, they should not be used merely to beat the Egyptian censorship. The absurdity of their use for the Noyes Thomas story is clearly indicated by the fact that he was flying home shortly afterwards and could have written his story in his own office.

I hope you do not find this lengthy note boring but I do feel it is necessary for us to examine the question in detail and formulate correct rules on the use of the Canal Zone communications.

Yours sincerely

[sgd] T.R. LITTLE

APPENDIX THREE

Letter from Tom Clayton dated 8 February 1953, the foreign correspondent for the *Daily Express* at the time.

Cairo February 8th, 1953

Dear Colonel Hornby,

Here briefly is a written 'recap' of the events of the weekend of January 16/17. It is merely confirming my statement that you could quote me fully as, so to speak, your witness in any dispute which has arisen.

I would firstly like to go on record by refuting any suggestion that you may have unfairly favoured any one correspondent that weekend. On the contrary I (like all the other Express correspondents who have passed this way) have found you eminently fair and of the greatest assistance on all occasions.

I shall be writing to the C.O. of Army P.R. at War Office to say this more fully later this month.

But this is a summary of the events of that weekend from a correspondent's viewpoint. I and so far as I know all the RESIDENT Cairo correspondents 'sat tight' on the anti-coup story. There was a very definite censorship stop ordered one gathered by the junta. We then had to decide whether to recruit your aid in getting the story to London by the Fayid cablehead or not.

I decided against it as I understand did the other resident correspondents. This was why: we were dealing with one hot news story concerning purely Egyptian domestic politics. If the Egyptians discovered correspondents had used Fayid to evade censorship they would then have a good case for a diplomatic protest.

As all names and passport details etc. are registered at check points along the Suez and Ismailia roads it would have been easy even for

Egyptian Intelligence to put two and two together had stories appeared in the London papers with too much accurate detail.

Then Rodin slipped away and used that cablehead. He was only on a short visit to Egypt and had not the same interest as the resident men in preserving the Fayid facilities for some future date. I am therefore not quarreling at all with his action. But when Rodin went to the Canal Zone and returned THE SAME DAY it was apparent to me at least that if the Egyptians protested then the Foreign Office might have banned our using it in the future.

I like other correspondents have found it extremely useful for filing background information and stories for interpretive use in London. But the Fayid cablehead has been used discreetly in the past. None of the stories going out by that route have been dateline Cairo or carry any indication that they originated from the Staff correspondent in Cairo.

In view of the fact that this cablehead may be vital one day in the not too distant future to resident correspondents for getting across a British angle on events here – as during the Zone troubles – this situation was put to you by me. I was seeking some ruling which would safeguard a discreet use of the Fayid facilities.

I had discussed it with several correspondents, notably Tom Little, senior of the resident men, before doing so. I understand from you that one correspondent says he was not consulted. That is as maybe, but I still think some definite rule such as saying that the time is inopportune, as I think it was that weekend, for using it. I do not of course suggest that the Army should set itself up as a censor of messages; far from it. But on certain occasions the Fayid facility should be closed to a specific story as that weekend. I realize that this is extremely difficult to decide. I am very much concerned the facility should not be lost forever.

But I am saying in writing now what I have previously said in words to you. It was as I then thought – and still do – the general opinion that Rodin who was simply doing his job as a visiting correspondent in getting the story out as best he could had endangered the Fayid facility for us all.

Far from you having favoured any one correspondent it was simply that you felt you were acting in the interests of all in passing on the facts I have briefly outlined to Fayid H.Q. I am of course hoping that we shall one day shortly be able to return to a discreet use of the cablehead once all this business is sorted out. The issue was of course further complicated by the fact that two correspondents in the Zone were cabling Cairo stories from there. That is none of my business; they were in the Zone. I repeat that I do not want the Egyptians to tumble to the fact that the Fayid cablehead is being used by correspondents here in Cairo. Nor will they if things are done discreetly as they always have I understand from correspondents who have been here longer than I in the past.

It is a difficult situation to express clearly in writing. I am hoping that this letter which, though a private letter to you is for any at H.Q. to see if you wish, will make it clear that I do not subscribe to the suggestion that you acted other than in what you thought was the best interests of ALL correspondents. In fact you were acting on the advice of correspondents – and I thought at the time I was expressing a general view of all resident correspondents.

I shall be quite happy to amplify or clarify any points when I next visit the Zone with Col. Carroll.

APPENDIX FOUR

Extract from letter to the Foreign Office, London, written by Ambassador Sir Ralph Stevenson.

British Embassy
Cairo

7th February, 1952

[Dear Jack]

1. For reasons which you will readily appreciate I have been unable to report on information work at this post until now. As the dismissal of the Wafd Government on 27th January, and its replacement by Ali Maher's new government of Independents, marks a definite period in the evolution of Anglo-Egyptian relations there is obvious advantage in extending the period to cover the month of January. I therefore deal in this report with the work of the Information Department from 1st October to 31st January.

2. On Monday the 6th October, when Nahas Pasha tabled his original decrees denouncing the Anglo-Egyptian Treaty of 1936 and annexing the Sudan to Egypt, the bulk of the Embassy was still in Alexandria. As Cairo remains the centre of Egyptian journalism summer and winter alike the entire Information Department was there. The only means of communication, other than the D.W.S., which was already operating above capacity, was the telephone; and from the beginning of the crisis the Alexandria – Cairo trunk line was unreliable, often inaudible and at all times laible to lengthy delays. Until the Embassy's return from Alexandria on 18th October, therefore, the Information Department had to use their commonsense and often to take snap decisions on their own responsibility.

3. In addition to maintaining its regional output and keeping alive such friendly contact with the Egyptian press as was possible in the circumstances the Department's first task was to cope with the horde

of foreign correspondents which descended on Cairo immediately after abrogation. Parkes decided that the only way of dealing with this influx was to hold regular press conferences. He held the first conference, which was attended by 37 correspondents (to avoid the conference degenerating into a slanging match Egyptians have never been invited) on 8th October. Since that date the Department has held 130 conferences. For a fortnight following the incidents at Ismailia on 16th October conferences were held twice a day. Apart from this the only days on which a conference has not been held are 25th December and 26th and 27th January. On these latter two days the Department was on hand to deal with individual callers and answer telephone enquiries but few correspondents were able to make their way to the Embassy. Some indeed had been burnt out in Shepheards Hotel. The total number of correspondents who have attended these conferences is 113, and 16 different nationalities have been represented.

4. Some of those press conferences have been critical, notably those following the Kafr Abdou operation and the disarming of the Ismailia police, and at times when the telephonic communication with Fayid and Moascar has been bad the Department has had to make, and avoid dropping, bricks with an unsatisfactory modicum of straw. The last three weeks have been particularly difficult since the Egyptians severed telephonic communication with the Zone and we had to rely on our R.T. link exclusively. But everyone has kept their temper and the atmosphere has been one of friendliness and mutual understanding throughout, and I am satisfied that these conferences, which continue to be very fully attended, have played a useful part in obtaining for us a not unsympathetic world press. Here I should like to record my appreciation of the services of Lt. Col. Hornby, A.D.P.R., B.T.E., stationed in Cairo, who joined the staff of the department as an Assistant Military Attaché shortly after abrogation. Despite the anxiety inherent in his anomalous position – for five weeks he and his family were without diplomatic identity documents and even passports – this officer has throughout worked unsparingly to provide a full service of news events in the Canal Zone and their interpretation. The success of these conferences is due in large measure to his efforts............

Bibliography

Artemis Cooper, *Cairo in the War*, Hamish Hamilton, 1989

Randolph S. Churchill, *Youth, 1874-1900*, William Heinemann, 1966

Winston S. Churchill, *The River War*, Eyre & Spottiswoode, 1933

Mohammed Heikel-Nasser, *The Cairo Documents*, New English Library

Robert Hornby, *The Press in Modern Society*, Frederick Muller, 1965

Elspeth Huxley, *Nine Faces of Kenya*, Collins Harvill, 1990

Joachim Joeston, *Nasser, The Rise to Power*, Odhams Press, 1960

Tom Little, *Egypt*, Ernest Benn, 1958

Harold Macmillan, *The Tide of Fortune, 1945-1955*, Thomson Newspapers

Barry St Clare McBride, *Farouk of Egypt,* Robert Hale, 1967

Mohammed Neguib, *Egypt's Destiny,* Victor Gollancz Ltd, 1955

Alfred Sansom, *I Spied Spies,* George Harrap & Co., 1965

Max Rodenbeck, *Cairo, The City Victorious,* Picador, 1988

Anwar Sadat, *Revolt on the Nile,* Allan Wingate, 1957

Anwar Sadat, *In Search of Identity,* Harper Row, 1977

Jehan Sadat, *Woman of Egypt,* Bloomsbury Publishing Ltd, 1987

Index